Cambridge Elements

Elements in International Relations
edited by
Jon C. W. Pevehouse
University of Wisconsin–Madison
Tanja A. Börzel
Freie Universität Berlin
Edward D. Mansfield
University of Pennsylvania

ENVIRONMENTAL ETHICS OF WAR

Tamar Meisels
Tel Aviv University

CAMBRIDGE
UNIVERSITY PRESS

Shaftesbury Road, Cambridge CB2 8EA, United Kingdom

One Liberty Plaza, 20th Floor, New York, NY 10006, USA

477 Williamstown Road, Port Melbourne, VIC 3207, Australia

314–321, 3rd Floor, Plot 3, Splendor Forum, Jasola District Centre, New Delhi – 110025, India

103 Penang Road, #05–06/07, Visioncrest Commercial, Singapore 238467

Cambridge University Press is part of Cambridge University Press & Assessment, a department of the University of Cambridge.

We share the University's mission to contribute to society through the pursuit of education, learning and research at the highest international levels of excellence.

www.cambridge.org
Information on this title: www.cambridge.org/9781009622714

DOI: 10.1017/9781009622684

© Tamar Meisels 2025

This publication is in copyright. Subject to statutory exception and to the provisions of relevant collective licensing agreements, no reproduction of any part may take place without the written permission of Cambridge University Press & Assessment.

When citing this work, please include a reference to the DOI 10.1017/9781009622684

First published 2025

A catalogue record for this publication is available from the British Library

ISBN 978-1-009-62271-4 Hardback
ISBN 978-1-009-62269-1 Paperback
ISSN 2515-706X (online)
ISSN 2515-7302 (print)

Cambridge University Press & Assessment has no responsibility for the persistence or accuracy of URLs for external or third-party internet websites referred to in this publication and does not guarantee that any content on such websites is, or will remain, accurate or appropriate.

Environmental Ethics of War

Elements in International Relations

DOI: 10.1017/9781009622684
First published online: March 2025

Tamar Meisels
Tel Aviv University

Author for correspondence: Tamar Meisels, meisels@tauex.tau.ac.il

Abstract: War is bad for nature, yet relatively little attention has been devoted to environmental military ethics by just war theorists and philosophers of war. Most wars since 1945 have been civil conflicts, often in areas containing the greatest biodiversity. Combining environmental ethics with ethics of war, this Element examines how the environmental crisis should challenge and change the rules of war. While environmental wartime regulation has been addressed rarely by just war theorists, environmental *jus ad bellum* has hardly been tackled at all. Can environmental harm trigger a new justification for war? Can targeting nature constitute terrorism? And what would be a proportionate response to 'environmental aggression'? With global degradation and climate change right around the corner, this Element discusses some of the most pressing practical ethics issues of our times, suggesting that grave environmental transgressions should be combatted by measures that do not themselves cause disproportionate harm to nature.

Keywords: just war theory, military ethics, natural environment, revisionist philosophy of war, terrorism

© Tamar Meisels 2025

ISBNs: 9781009622714 (HB), 9781009622691 (PB), 9781009622684 (OC)
ISSNs: 2515-706X (online), 2515-7302 (print)

Contents

Introduction   1

1 Protecting the Natural Environment during Armed
  Conflict: Environmental *Jus in Bello*   7

2 Environmental Just Wars: *Jus ad Bellum* and the
  Natural Environment   20

3 Environmental Ethics in Civil Wars   38

4 Environmental Terrorism   49

  References   65

Introduction

Recent decades have witnessed unprecedented environmental deterioration, with climate change and extreme weather events, such as floods and droughts, posing significant challenges. The scientific consensus points to mankind as the main culprit, as well as the sole cause capable of moral agency. The unprecedented increase in human population alongside a variety of polluting enterprises – industry, technology, and urban development – harm wilderness areas, contributing to the extinction of biological species and threatening their present and future generations.

Of all human activities, however, warfare has a particularly significant and enduring effect on the natural environment, with militaries generating exceptionally large carbon footprints, both in war and in peacetime.[1] According to one authority, 'collectively the world's militaries are estimated to be the largest single polluter on Earth, accounting for as much as 20 percent of all global environmental degradation'.[2]

Training and preparing for war, as well as fighting and recovering from it, inevitably have negative effects on natural systems. Maintaining, exercising, and mobilizing standing armies contribute to carbon emissions. Military industries cause extensive pollution; warfare disrupts ecosystems, harms wilderness areas, and jeopardizes biodiversity.[3] As for the instigation of war, conflict over natural resources (scarce or abundant) is a common cause of civil wars; and their conduct, often within biodiversity hotspots, is particularly damaging to the natural environment and its inhabitants.[4] Moreover, studies indicate that environmental degradation may well increase the incidence of armed conflict, particularly of the non-international variety.[5]

Undeniably, in atypical cases conflicts or their aftermath may have beneficial effects on the environment, such as removing people from an entire area, leaving nature to bloom, and wildlife to roam freely. This is, however, the rare exception that proves the rule.[6] Overwhelmingly, warfare is very bad for our natural environment, and modern warfare is especially so.

The adverse effects of military activity are evident even before hostilities break out, and often endure in their aftermath. Most notably perhaps, in light of timely concerns, is the potential of environmental harm caused by war to

---

[1] Machlis and Hanson, 2008: 729; Woods, 2007: 19–20, 29–30.   [2] Woods, 2007: 20.
[3] Hanson, 2018: 50; Machlis and Hanson, 2008.
[4] Dudley et al., 2002: 323; Hourcle, 2001: 653, 661, 679–80; Machlis and Hanson, 2008: 731; Milburn and Van Goozen, 2021: 659; Roberts, 2000: 75–77.
[5] Dudley, 2002: 324; Homer-Dixon, 1991: 76–116; 1994: 5–40.
[6] Dudley et al., 2002: 319–20; Hanson, 2018: 50, 51, 56, 57, 58; Johnston, 2015: sec. 2; Milburn and Van Goozen, 2021: 658.

increase worldwide refugee crises and widespread epidemics *post bellum* (after war), alongside the large-scale economic disruptions that accompany both.[7] The Spanish influenza pandemic that followed World War I is a case in point. Moreover, as with environmental concerns more generally, some wartime damage will also have multi-generational effects.

Bearing in mind the climate crisis along with the ecological footprint of military enterprises, environmental concerns must now be incorporated into the moral evaluation of violent conflict. To this end, this Element integrates two branches of applied ethics rarely studied in tandem – namely environmental ethics and the ethics of war, as well as law and general moral philosophies – and considers their combined impact on environmental wartime issues. It suggests that considerations arising from environmental ethics should inform contemporary just war theory and its agenda, introducing and addressing the uncharted territory of the environmental ethics of armed conflict.

Several themes are developed in the Element. First, the concept of an environmental morality of war breaks new ground and, as such, ought to build carefully on the wide range of relevant theories in ethics of war, environmental ethics, law, and moral philosophy. International law already contains some prohibitions and restrictions on militaries for protecting nature during armed conflict, supplying the primary building blocks for thinking about environmental obligations in wartime. Ethics is different from law, however, in depth and scope – less technical and unhindered by practical considerations of implementation, international ramifications, and compromises – and should step in to develop the wartime protection of nature.[8]

Beyond military ethics, planetary changes suggest that grave environmental harm may generate a new 'just cause' for war, contra existing international law. The relative frequency of civil conflicts and their common location in bio-sensitive regions is a further source of environmental concern.[9] Finally, 'environmental terrorism' is a new and ambiguous label, requiring classification and moral evaluation. Wartime proportionality and sincere intention to protect nature suggest countering 'environmental aggression', terroristic or otherwise, via measures short of full-scale conflict, avoiding excessively ruinous consequences not only to humans and other animals but also to their natural surroundings.

---

[7] Woods, 2007: 20.

[8] Reichberg and Syse, 2000: 451. On these differences between law and moral philosophy, see also Waldron, 2010: 92–93.

[9] Dudley et al., 2002: 323; Hourcle, 2001: 653, 661, 679–80; Machlis and Hanson, 2008: 731; Milburn and Van Goozen, 2021: 598; Roberts, 2000: 75–77.

Historically, war has always been destructive for the environment. Nevertheless, the issue of protecting nature per se from the deleterious effects of warfare surfaced only in the late twentieth century, due mostly to the unprecedented environmental devastation caused by the Vietnam and Gulf wars.[10] Since that time, increasing evidence of environmental damage caused by armed conflict has attracted academic attention, much of which remains empirical and dispersed among different disciplines, ranging from political science and international relations to ecology, law, and military history.[11]

In contrast to lawyers and empirical researchers, just war theorists and philosophers of war have yet to step up to the plate. Their voluminous philosophical accounts of the morality of war in recent decades have paid virtually no attention to the ethical issues raised by damage to the natural environment whether before, during, or after armed conflict.[12] On the whole, the military ethics, or 'morality of war', perspective on the environmental damage inflicted by armed forces is glaringly absent, as is any discussion of the environmental causes of war.

Building on the exceptional literature in the field, this Element takes one small step towards remedying the deficiency. The four sections offer initial methods and content in promoting the incorporation of environmental considerations in contemporary scholarship on the morality of war. This is an absolute necessity for any twenty-first-century ethics of war and its regulations, with implications for both *jus ad bellum* (the legitimacy of engaging in war) and *jus in bello* (just conduct in war), as well as any future discussion of *jus para bellum* (the just preparation for war, in which, for example, military training might damage the environment) and *jus post bellum* (justice after war).[13]

Section 1 lays the groundwork for some of the overarching proposals expressed throughout the Element. I begin by briefly surveying the existing philosophical literature on environmental justice in wartime (environmental *jus in bello*). Combining environmental ethics with the ethics of war, the Element asks how the environmental crisis should challenge and change the rules of engagement in war, stressing the need for ethical guidelines in this field. What would a 'greener' ethics of war look like?

---

[10] Hedahl et al., 2017: 432; Johnston, 2015: sec. 2; Reichberg and Syse, 2000: 449; Schmitt, 1996: 239–40; Westing, 1983.

[11] Machlis and Hanson, 2008: 729.

[12] Pioneering exceptions, reviewed in Section 1, include Drucker, 1989; Esteve, 2020; Hedahl et al., 2017; Johnston, 2015; Milburn and Goozen, 2020; Reichberg and Syse, 2000; Woods, 2007.

[13] For accounts of *jus para* and *post bellum* – right conduct in preparation for and aftermath of war – regarding the environment, see Drucker, 1989, 140–43; Hedahl et al., 2017, 337–40; Roberts, 2000, 84.

My point of departure is the International Law of Armed Conflict (ILOAC), identifying the most directly relevant existing environmental regulations in wartime applicable to international armed conflict. Unlike moral philosophers, lawyers have of necessity already paid notable normative attention to environmental regulation in wartime, 'jump-starting' moral philosophy, as it were. Humanitarian law, legal commentary, academic analysis, and critique of existing environmental regulations in armed conflict should supply moral philosophers with the initial material that stimulates further elaboration. Perhaps counter-intuitively, I argue that environmental protection in war is an issue in which ethics must take its cue from the law rather than vice versa.[14]

Beyond law, a good place to begin a new moral inquiry is the point of convergence of the various philosophies and world-views that pertain to this issue. This principal suggestion, as developed in Section 1, does not look to the law as a mechanism for settling disagreements, and is distinct from compromise between opposing world-views. Instead, it suggests something like an 'overlapping consensus', a moment of agreement (as opposed to compromise) between vastly different perspectives.[15]

Thinking comprehensively about environmental protection in wartime requires consideration of contesting viewpoints within environmental ethics (human versus non-human perspectives), various moral philosophies, and competing just war traditions. When these very different roads all lead to the same moral conclusion, Section 1 suggests that this conclusion is most likely to be correct. Attaining mutual moral ground also serves to prevent extremism or unrealistic idealism in any one perspective, advancing practical ethics.

Finally, with these foundations in hand, the section raises and critiques the proposal to grant nature civilian status in wartime. Rejecting as untenable the extreme attribution of absolute non-combatant immunity for the non-human world, it supports a more moderate proposal to weigh harm to the natural environment on the cost side of wartime proportionality calculations, beyond damage to purely human resources and surroundings.[16] This would mean that foreseeably excessive harm to nature might place the legitimacy of an attack into question. This proposal is not far from emerging international norms, particularly international criminal law, and is, arguably, in keeping with overlapping consensus.[17]

---

[14] See Waldron, 2010: 87–88, on civilian immunity.
[15] Compare Rawls, 2005: lectures IV and V, 158–69; Reichberg and Syse, 2000: 452–53.
[16] Hedahl et al., 2017: 437.
[17] Rome Statute of the International Criminal Court, 19 July 1998, Article 8(2)(b)(iv), entered into force 1 July 2002. It is a war crime to intentionally launch an attack in the knowledge that the attack will cause not only incidental harm to human civilians, injury, and damage human objects but also 'widespread, long-term, and severe damage to the natural environment which would be

While the wartime status of nature and environmental wartime regulation during armed conflict (environmental *jus in bello*) have been addressed only rarely by just war theorists and moral philosophers, the environmental conditions under which states may legitimately resort to war or armed force (environmental *jus ad bellum*) have hardly been tackled at all. Moreover, because the law focuses invariably on rules mitigating the conduct of hostilities rather than on objective justice of cause, environmental *jus ad bellum* has been explored even less extensively than environmental *jus in bello*, in law as well as morality.

Can environmental harm trigger a new justification for war? What would be a proportionate response to 'environmental aggression'? Section 2 takes on these emerging challenges. Setting out with the presumption against the use of force and its exceptions, this section considers whether environmental harm can generate a new *casus belli*, a just cause or occasion for war, and what might be a proportionate response to aggressive or negligent harm to nature. Force is clearly justified against military attacks. Where environmental harm is not caused by military aggression, Section 2 argues, proportionality points towards counter-measures short of war. Responding in ways that minimize harm to nature also helps demonstrate a 'right intention' to combat environmental wrongs.

Section 3 suggests focusing any new 'environmental ethics of war' initially on Non-International Armed Conflict (NIAC), which has mostly been neglected by the just war tradition in all its aspects. This neglect overlaps with just war theory's neglect of the environment. Crucially, for our purposes, regions prone to civil conflict often contain the greatest biodiversity. Moreover, NIAC has also been the most common type of warfare since World War II. Consequently, fruitful inquiry into the new environmental ethics of war requires not only understanding the links between war and the natural environment but also paying special attention to the contexts and locations in which the majority of conflicts occur.

As in the previous sections, in Section 3 the law is both lacking and at the same time our best shot. Article 3 common to the Geneva Conventions (1949) and Additional Protocol II to the Geneva Conventions (1977) apply minimal humanitarian provisions to NIAC.[18] Notwithstanding, lawyers note that most

---

clearly excessive in relation to the direct overall military advantage anticipated'. See also Protocol Additional to the Geneva Conventions of 12 August 1949, and Relating to the Protection of Victims of International Armed Conflicts (Protocol I), 8 June 1977, Article 35(3), entered into force 7 December 1978, which directly prohibits methods and means of warfare intended or expected to 'cause widespread, long-term, and severe damage to the natural environment', without granting nature full civilian status.

[18] Convention (III) Relative to the Treatment of Prisoners of War, Geneva, 12 August 1949: Conflicts Not of an International Character, Article 3; Protocol Additional to the Geneva

laws of armed conflict (LOAC) do not apply to NIAC; and when it comes to the environment, restrictions are virtually non-existent.[19] This is particularly troublesome, as noted, in view of the relative frequency of internal conflicts as well as their prevalence in biodiversity hotspots.[20] Nonetheless, Section 3 re-emphasizes that a new ethical aspect of armed conflict – in this case the virtually non-existent environmental regulation of NIAC – is best built on pre-existing legal understandings, even if these are not, strictly speaking, directly applicable to NIAC from a LOAC perspective.

Morally, Section 3 argues for the existence of special obligations on the part of both governments and rebels in all civil conflicts – fiduciary duties of care – towards the populations whom they purport to represent and propose to govern, including their natural surroundings. From a non-cosmopolitan perspective, both insurgents and soldiers have special obligations stemming from national affiliations and partiality towards fellow citizens and their homeland terrain. Finally, universal obligations require everyone to pay special attention to biodiversity conservation in armed conflict, particularly in biologically rich regions. The reality of civil conflict is, of course, very different.

Last, Section 4 examines the relatively new label 'environmental terrorism'. In keeping with the theme of this Element, this conceptual analysis combines theoretical insights from both terrorism scholarship and environmental politics and ethics. Arson attacks launched from Gaza to Israel, burning fields and forests (2018–23), present the primary contemporary example; the section also contains some references to the October 7 massacre that followed. Relatedly, terrorism usually denotes the murder of civilians. Notwithstanding, I argue that the severity of attacks against the natural environment should not be underestimated, and may sometimes go far enough towards threatening non-combatants to constitute bona fide terrorism.

Completing and complementing the discussion on environmental aggression in Section 2, this final section considers appropriate responses to direct and intentional attacks on the non-human world. Even in the face of outright armed aggression against the natural environment, Section 4 concludes that proportionality prescribes a first resort to softer tactics, such as economic sanctions, followed by limited force short of war – *jus ad vim* – against primary culprits

---

Conventions of 12 August 1949, and Relating to the Protection of Victims of Non-International Armed Conflicts (Protocol II), 8 June 1977. These provisions aim to uphold civilian immunity and the rights of the sick and wounded, as well as prohibiting torture and further excesses in wartime.

[19] Bruch, 2001: 703, 709, 714–15; Burger, 1996: 337–38; Hourcle, 2001: 680; Meron, 1996: chap. XX; Roberts, 2000: 76–77.

[20] Hanson, 2018: 51; Hanson et al., 2009: 579–83; Milburn and Van Goozen, 2021: 659.

and their infrastructure, reserving full-scale armed conflict to combat graver invasions and assaults on human life and limb.

One final preliminary note on scope and range: this is a very short introductory work that throws a wide and global net in both its topic and its content. The cases addressed in this Element range all the way from civil wars in Africa to fires in the Amazon rainforest and incendiary kites and balloons sent from the Gaza Strip to southern Israel. In a century of great environmental concern and urgency, with global degradation and climate change right around the corner, this Element raises some of the most pressing practical issues of ethics in our times.

1 Protecting the Natural Environment during Armed Conflict: Environmental *Jus in Bello*

Warfare is among the greatest threats to natural systems, nearly always involving environmental destruction alongside human carnage.[21] Despite this, relatively little attention has been focused on environmental wartime issues either by advocates of the traditional ethics of war – 'just war theory' – or by contemporary moral philosophers.

However, there is a veritable gold mine of *legal* literature on environmental regulation during armed conflict and its aftermath. 'International law has not been silent on the environmental effects of military activity',[22] and neither have legal scholars.[23] In contrast to the litany of legal sources on emerging environmental standards in international law of armed conflict, the environmental ethics of war is extremely limited, with extraordinary exceptions reviewed in Subsection 1.2. In the sphere of wartime environmental protection, the law appears to have preceded moral scholarship and may serve to advance it.

1.1 Environmental Laws of War

The most directly relevant environmental restrictions in wartime, applicable to international armed conflicts, appear in the following legal documents, all of which remain primarily human-centred and utilitarian in their perspective.

- The 1959 Antarctic Treaty bans military tests and nuclear activity in the region, partly for ecological reasons.[24]

---

[21] Attfield, 2018: 75; Hourcle, 2001: 653–93.   [22] Drucker, 1989: 143.
[23] The list is extensive, e.g. Bruch, 2001; Cohan, 2002; Deiderich, 1992; Gardam, 2004: 132–33, 177–78; Green, 2018: 152–53, 155, 162–63, 183, 221, 374; Hourcle, 2001; Richards and Schmitt, 1999; Roberts, 1996: 222–27; 2000; Schmitt, 1996; 1997; Schwabach, 2000; Schwabach, 2003.
[24] Antarctic Treaty, 1 December 1959, Protocol on Environmental Protection, 4 October 1991, Articles 2–3, entered into force 14 January 1998.

- The 1977 Environmental Modification Techniques Convention (ENMOD) bars using the environment itself (i.e., changing or manipulating natural processes) as a weapon.[25]
- Protocol I, Addition to the Geneva Convention (GPI) 1977 – Article 35(3), proscribes 'methods and means of warfare intended or expected to cause widespread, long-term, and severe damage to the natural environment'. Article 55(1) repeats this and adds a further prohibition against damage to the natural environment that 'prejudice[s] the health or survival of the [human] population'.[26]
- 1980 Protocol III to the UN Convention, Article 2(4), prohibits targeting forests and other plant cover with incendiary weapons, except when such natural elements are used to hide or camouflage combatants or are themselves otherwise military targets.[27]
- Finally, the Rome Statute of the International Criminal Court, following the language of Protocol I, brands as a war crime: 'widespread, long-term, and severe damage to the natural environment which would be clearly excessive in relation to the direct overall military advantage anticipated'.[28]

Environmental legal protections also have multifarious sources and modes of application. International Environmental Law (IEL), such as the aforementioned 1959 Antarctic Treaty (and the 1982 UN Law of the Sea Convention),[29] offers direct protection to the environment, as does International Humanitarian Law (IHL) in Article 35(3) and Article 55(1) of Additional Protocol I. In addition, IHL offers indirect protection to the natural environment as in Protocol I, Article 54(2), whereby 'it is prohibited to attack, destroy, remove or render useless objects indispensable to the survival of the civilian population, such as foodstuffs, agricultural areas for the production of foodstuffs, crops, livestock, drinking water installations and supplies and irrigation works, for the specific purpose of

---

[25] Environmental Modification Convention (Convention on the Prohibition of Military or Any Other Hostile Use of Environmental Modification Techniques), 18 May 1977, entered into force 5 October 1978.
[26] Geneva Conventions, Protocol Additional to the Geneva Conventions of 12 August 1949, and Relating to the Protection of Victims of International Armed Conflicts (Protocol I), 8 June 1977, Articles 35(3), 55(1), entered into force 7 December 1978.
[27] Conventions on Prohibitions or Restrictions on the Use of Certain Weapons which may be deemed to be Excessively Injurious or to have Indiscriminate Effects (Protocol III), 10 October 1980, Article 2(4), entered into force 2 December 1983. (Less directly relevant, Protocol II to the same convention prohibits/restricts the use of landmines, booby-traps, and some other explosive devices.) See also Bruch, 2001: 710–11, on applicability to NIAC.
[28] Rome Statute of the International Criminal Court, 19 July 1998, Article 8(2)(b)(iv), entered into force 1 July 2002.
[29] United Nations Convention on the Law of the Sea (1982). Burger, 1996: 340, also notes the Basel Convention on the Control of Transboundary Movements of Hazardous Wastes and Their Disposal, which restricts the movements of hazardous wastes, applying to transport by air.

denying them for their sustenance value to the civilian population'.[30] International Criminal Law (ICL) – Article 8(2)(b)(iv) of the 1998 Rome Statute – makes various kinds of damage to, and destruction of, the natural environment a war crime.

In their 2000 article 'Protecting the Natural Environment in Wartime: Ethical Considerations from the Just War Tradition', one of the few ethical treatments of the subject, Gregory Reichberg and Henrik Syse point out that environmental protections in international law enjoy nothing like the absolute status that is attached to civilian immunity or the prohibition on torture, and (Protocol I and ENMOD notwithstanding) are couched largely in terms of necessity and proportionality.[31]

It is also noteworthy that the standard of the Rome Statute is manifestly weaker than that required in Additional Protocol I. In order to be prosecutable as a war crime, damage to the natural environment has to be not only 'widespread, long-term, and severe' but also 'clearly excessive in relation to the direct overall military advantage anticipated'.[32] This is a clear and typical example of environmental interdictions falling back on proportionality.[33] Nevertheless, as David Luban points out more generally, the discrepancies between Protocol I and the Rome Statute should not be read as lowering the standard of rightful conduct required of military organizations under the laws of war. Instead, they represent the difference between rightful conduct and a criminal offence: 'the drafters apparently thought that fairness to the accused requires a less stringent standard. It follows, however, that the Rome Statute's standard should not be taken to represent the standard of rightful conduct.'[34]

Furthermore, principles and provisions of the law of war that do not specifically refer to the 'environment', such as the aforementioned necessity and proportionality requirements as well as peacetime environmental law, may also add to its protection.[35] Legal protection afforded to 'cultural property' and 'World Heritage Sites' might contribute towards safeguarding the environment in specific areas.[36] Conventions such as the aforementioned 1982 UN Law of the Sea Convention, obliging states to protect and preserve the marine

---

[30] Protocol I, Article 54(2), https://ihl-databases.icrc.org/en/ihl-treaties/api-1977/article-54.
[31] Reichberg and Syse, 2000: 450; Schmitt, 1996: 245–50.
[32] Dinstein, 2004: 120, on the addition of the adverb 'clearly'; Luban, 2013: 296.
[33] Reichberg and Syse, 2000: 450; Schmitt, 1996: 95.
[34] Luban, 2013: 297, regarding proportionality.
[35] Bruch, 2001: 710; Meron, 1996: 353, 356; Roberts, 2000; Schmitt, 1997.
[36] Bruch, 2001: 711–13, with reference to the Hague Cultural Property Convention (1954) and World Heritage Convention (1972). On 'World Heritage Sites', see also Fabre, 2021. Whether protecting natural 'World Heritage Sites' of great environmental value, such as the Amazon rainforest, could ever justify going to war is the topic of Subsection 1.2, though there is no legal basis for war on such grounds.

environment (Article 192) and to prevent and reduce its pollution (Article 194), are (arguably) applicable to military commanders at sea.[37] Finally, leading militaries and international organizations now pay at least cursory attention to environmental issues in their handbooks and directives.[38]

Law is by no means an unusual starting point for ethical analysis of war. Current scholarship on the ethics of war is, however, deeply philosophical, largely concerned with the underlying principles of morality rather than with concrete practicable rules. Notwithstanding, the just war tradition has always been intertwined with legal thinking ('natural law') and the subsequent emergence of international laws of war.[39] Contemporary environmental concerns should be no exception.

Moreover, where law imposes normative regulation in the face of practical necessity before deep moral reflection has developed, 'law is a school of moral philosophy'.[40] Discussing civilian immunity, Jeremy Waldron makes this point:

> law often colonizes an area of normative inquiry first, before serious moral inquiry, as we know it begins. Often, we learn how to moralize by learning how to ask and answer legalistic questions: I strongly believe that law is a school of moral philosophy. Historically, this has been particularly true of the laws and customs of armed conflict.[41]

Referring to the law as a guide to ethics is especially noteworthy in the case of wartime environmental protection because law and legal experts have already paid systematic attention to this issue, whereas moral philosophers, for the most part, have not. Commentary and critique of environmental regulations in armed conflict should supply philosophers with normative food for thought, but they also leave much work to do. Ethics is wider and more inclusive than law, especially international law, which often represents a minimal compromise between states rather than deep moral reflections about war.[42] Moreover, law and lawyers concentrate on *jus in bello*, the rules of engagement in international armed conflict, discussed in this section. They have less to say about further environmental aspects of war addressed in the remainder of the Element. Law has a necessary practical focus. Considerations of technicalities and implementation may restrain and limit legal sources, in contrast with deep moral theory or comprehensive philosophical evaluation of environmental ethics in wartime

---

[37] See note 9. United Nations Convention on the Law of the Sea (1982); Burger, 1996: 340.
[38] Burger, 1996: 333–45; Meron, 1996: 353–58. See also Schmitt, 1996: 243–44, on environmental directives in military manuals.
[39] Reichberg and Syse, 2000: 450; Waldron, 2010: 88.
[40] Waldron, 2010: 87. In addition to the aforementioned laws that offer some environmental wartime protection, Milburn and Van Goozen, 2023: 437, point out that 'IHL is ahead of JWT on Animal inclusion'.
[41] Waldron, 2010: 87. [42] Reichberg and Syse, 2000: 451.

that is sorely lacking.[43] In the case in hand, as we have seen, law is necessarily and exclusively human centred, and its environmental provisions are non-absolute;[44] environmental ethics incorporates other perspectives as well. Here it is clear that ethical inquiry should deepen, explain, and widen the scope of environmental wartime issues raised in the surrounding legal literature.[45]

1.2 Environmental Military Ethics

Falling far behind their legal counterparts, moral philosophers have paid scant attention to environmental ramifications of military activity, rendering 'environmental considerations ... peripheral in analyses of the ethics of war'.[46] Notable philosophical exceptions reviewed here are few and far between, and their authors may well be regarded as pioneers in their field. Some of these contributions adopt a highly specific approach, while others offer a more general ethical analysis. Merrit Drucker (1989) discusses a military commander's professional responsibility for the natural environment in both peacetime and wartime, arguing from environmental ethics that military necessity cannot justify any extent of environmental devastation. Most interestingly, Drucker aspires to attribute non-combatant status to the environment itself and its non-human natural inhabitants. Focusing on environmental protection, such as immunity for nature in wartime, however, risks losing sight of humanitarian concern for the lives of soldiers and civilians.[47]

Drawing on Drucker's analysis, Reichberg and Syse (2000) are the first contemporary just war theorists to explicitly suggest incorporating environmental considerations in the moral assessment of war and its conduct. Focusing specifically on Thomas Aquinas's influential formulation of the just war requirements and natural law, along with his conception of the relationship between humanity and nature in terms of responsibility and stewardship, the authors suggest that the just war tradition 'provides an ethical vocabulary for assessing the impact of war on our natural environment'.[48]

Combining some of these previous insights, Mark Woods (2007) recommends introducing environmental ethics into the just war tradition and

---

[43] Reichberg and Syse, 2000: 451; Waldron, 2010: 92–93.
[44] Reichberg and Syse, 2000: 450; Schmitt, 1996: 245–50.
[45] Compare Reichberg and Syse, 2000. Recognizing that IHL preceded JWT on animal inclusion, Milburn and Van Goozen, 2023: 437, also note the need and space for moral philosophy to expand on legal thinking; for example: 'international lawyers may find themselves constrained in important ways by existing (highly anthropocentric) legal frameworks, in a way that philosophers need not be'.
[46] Hedahl et al., 2017: 431.
[47] Deiderich, 1992: 156–57; Richards and Schmitt, 1999: 1088–91, especially 1090; Roberts, 1996: 268; 2000: 81.
[48] Reichberg and Syse, 2000: 449, 457–58, 466.

considers how this might be done.[49] Like Drucker, Woods denies that military necessity always trumps environmental considerations and poses a vital practical ethics question: to what extent, if any, can we require armies and military commanders to put their mission and men at risk in order to avoid environmental harm?[50] Rejecting the traditionally stark distinction between *jus ad bellum–jus in bello* and the independence of the rules of conduct from just cause, Woods's environmental standards suggest that a war likely to involve significant attacks on nature would be *ipso facto* unjust, regardless of cause, and would necessarily fail *ad bellum* criteria such as proportionality and competent authority.[51]

Next, Marcus Hedahl, Scott Clark, and Michael Beggins (2017), of the US Navy, argue that environmental change must affect the theoretical framework of the just war tradition at its very core, explicating this at both its *ad bellum* and *in bello* levels, as well as justice prior to and *post bellum*.[52] (I return to their discussion of *jus ad bellum* in Subsection 1.3.) Meanwhile, Laurie Johnston (2015) offers a religious account, based on the Christian virtues of humility and solidarity.[53]

Reflecting on the classics, Adrien Estève (2020) cites consequentialist–utilitarian arguments within the just war tradition for protecting the natural environment in times of war, complementing them with reasoning from virtue ethics.[54] Most recently, Josh Milburn and Sara Van Goozen (2021, 2023) focus exclusively on animal rights, partly in connection with the wartime requirements of necessity and proportionality, arguing plausibly that we ought to take into account wartime harm to individual animals when assessing the justice of military action.[55]

This invaluable collection of original analyses constitutes the latest ethical–philosophical discussion about war and the environment, leaving room for further thought on environmental *jus in bello*.

Pushing forward, ethical inquiry in this new area ought to set out from solid beginnings, those that generate the strongest consensus between competing moral theories and ethical standpoints. John Rawls famously coined the term 'overlapping consensus' to denote widespread agreement among free and equal citizens who espouse conflicting comprehensive doctrines on the principles of justice. This means that similar normative conclusions can be derived from

---

[49] Woods, 2007. [50] Woods, 2007: 17–18, 25.
[51] Woods, 2007: 26–29; cf. Reichberg and Syse, 2000.
[52] Hedahl et al., 2017. On *jus ad bellum*, see also Hedahl and Fruh, 2019. [53] Johnston, 2015.
[54] Estève, 2020.
[55] Milburn and Van Goozen, 2021: 657, with reference on p. 660 to Fabre, 2012.

different, even contrasting, philosophical and moral creeds, generating wide agreement from vastly different viewpoints.[56]

The idea of attaining overlapping consensus on environmental protection in wartime was first introduced by Reichberg and Syse in an attempt to reach beyond their specifically Thomist argument: 'Even if one discards the way of viewing man and nature outlined here, one may nonetheless accept it as one way of grounding a moral view of the environment and warfare.'[57]

This possibility of finding common moral ground, distinct from compromise, sustaining and supporting similar prescriptions from very different doctrines and perspectives – highly relevant to Reichberg and Syse's arguments from Thomas Aquinas – is wholly essential to the argument presented here. Thinking comprehensively about environmental protection in wartime requires contending with contesting points of view within environmental ethics, moral philosophy, and the just war tradition. There are, to date, at least three different perspectives in environmental ethics (anthropocentric, biocentric, and ecocentric), three relevant moral philosophies (utilitarian, deontological, and virtue ethics), and two prominent reigning theories of just war ('traditionalist' and 'revisionist'). It is impossible to explicate all these theories here, or to take sides in these divides, but it is important to note them. In the remainder of this section, I introduce traditional just war theory and its revisionist alternative, as well as very basic environmental ethics. Readers familiar with standard ethical theories on war and the environment (and the overlapping consensus strategy) may wish to skip ahead to Subsection 1.3.

Beginning in the medieval writings of Augustine and later of Thomas Aquinas, the definitive account of the just war tradition, or 'Just War Theory' (JWT), in modern times appears in Michael Walzer's classic *Just and Unjust Wars* and is closely aligned with the International Law of Armed Conflict (ILOAC). Within this tradition, the rules and customs of war divide sharply into two distinct categories: *jus ad bellum* governs the initial resort to war, and is the responsibility of state leaders, while *jus in bello* regulates the conduct of war by the military. Armies are required to distinguish civilians from combatants and to refrain from targeting the former. Combatants may fight and kill, regardless of the justness of their cause, and are legitimate targets of attack by virtue of their threatening nature. Non-combatants remain immune from direct

---

[56] Rawls, 2005: lectures IV and V, 158–69.
[57] Reichberg and Syse, 2000: 452–53. See also Woods, 2007: 24, appealing to a wide and varied audience. Admittedly (and somewhat anecdotally), Rawls himself may not have endorsed his method in this context. As Peter Singer points out critically: 'John Rawls has denied animals a place in his theory of justice, arguing that we owe justice only to those who have the concept of justice (except that we owe it to infant humans).' Singer, 1980: 325–37, esp. from sec. II, 328–37, 329; see also Rawls, 1971, sec. 77).

attack. Necessity precludes wanton violence. Proportionality *in bello* requires the military to minimize incidental harm to civilians and civilian objects.[58] These rules apply equally to all parties, independently of their respective causes and the overall justness of their war or any personal blame.[59]

Originating in the work of Jeff McMahan, the 'revisionist' morality of war takes issue with blanket civilian immunity, combatant equality, and the overarching independence of *jus in bello* from *jus ad bellum*. With its roots in the writings of Renaissance philosophers such as Francisco de Vitoria and Francisco Suarez in the sixteenth and seventeenth centuries, revisionist (neoclassical) theory denies that the existing rules and customs of war reflect deep morality. Ultimately, the reasons for fighting a war (whether just or unjust, defensive or aggressive) are inseparable from the very licence to fight and kill. Accordingly, just and unjust combatants cannot be morally equal. If killing in war is justified as self-defence, then only soldiers on the defensive side can possess this license. Moreover, combatants who fight an unjust war can rarely fulfill the *jus in bello* requirements of necessity and proportionality. (If their war is aggressive, futile, and injurious, how can any of its measures be necessary and proportionate?) Consequently, unjust wars also defy the laws that govern conduct in battle. Finally, not all civilians are innocent or non-threatening, so there can be no deep moral justification for their automatic immunity as a group. Liability to harm and immunity from harm, McMahan argues, should be determined on the basis of individual contribution to and responsibility for injustice, as in civilian life.[60]

The result is a well-known split within JWT and the emergence of two camps.[61] Much of the current scholarship on the ethics of war is of the critical–revisionist variety, while the remainder is mostly traditionalist, as are the laws and military handbooks.[62] Environmental issues are typically absent from any of this philosophical work on war.[63]

---

[58] Hurka, 2005: 35; Protocol I, Article 51 (5) (b). [59] Walzer, 1977: 21.
[60] McMahan, 2009. [61] Lazar, 2017.
[62] Contemporary revisionists notably include scholars such as Janina Dill, Cecile Fabre, Helen Frowe, Adil Haque, Gregory Reichberg, and David Rodin, to list but a few. It is both unnecessary and impossible to cite the vast literature in either camp, instead referring to Walzer and McMahan as archetypes. Taking a first step towards an animal-inclusive theory of the just war, Josh Milburn and Sara Van Goozen remain neutral in this split, maintaining plausibly that 'Revisionist and orthodox just-war theory ... can – and should – consider the effect of (just or unjust) combatants' actions on animals. Those with revisionist leanings are invited to assume that *in bello* examples below concern wars that are *ad bellum* just.' Milburn and Van Goozen, 2021: 662 n. 8, 665. Similar logic applies not only to JWT concerning animals, but to all conflicting moral perspectives that have a bearing on the environmental ethics of war.
[63] One recent prominent exception in the Revisionist camp is noteworthy but extremely limited: McMahan, 2020: 230–33, uses the brief example of 'climate war' to illustrate his discussion of population ethics and the 'non-identity problem'.

Environmental ethicists, for their part, are mostly uninvolved in this JWT debate. As for their own traditional divisions, broadly described, *anthropocentrism* regards the value of nature and its non-human components as solely instrumental in furthering human objectives. All living organisms, ecological compilations, and inanimate elements within nature are devoid of independent moral standing and are valuable solely for the benefit of mankind. *Biocentric* and *ecocentric* theories dispute this, and attribute intrinsic value and moral standing to non-human living individuals or ecological collectives, respectively. *Biocentrism*, literally signifying a 'life-centred' approach, grounds obligations for environmental protection in the moral value of other-than-human living individuals. By contrast, *ecocentrism* shifts the moral focus from individual creatures to ecological wholes, namely biological species, biomes, and entire ecosystems, and sanctions attaching intrinsic value to inanimate elements of the natural environment such as rivers, lakes, landscapes, and mountains.[64]

Beyond the anthropocentric versus non-anthropocentric (bio/ecocentric) divide, the three perspectives draw, in profoundly different ways, on general theories of normative ethics to establish humanity's moral obligation towards nature. Anthropocentric thinkers establish only *indirect* duties to protect the environment, based on the purely human interests of both current and future generations.[65] Such human-centred justifications for environmental protection, or combined approaches, rely on either virtue ethics, or utilitarianism, or deontology.[66]

Similarly, biocentric and ecocentric ethicists apply either utilitarian or deontological morality to make the case for the protection of non-human entities, grounding *direct* duties towards non-human moral subjects. Biocentric environmental ethics intersects with different general moral theories at various junctions, such as 'sentientism' – closely associated with Peter Singer's utilitarian approach to animal rights[67] – or 'biocentric consequentialism'[68] versus a deontological approach to animal rights.[69] Ecocentrism, ecological ethics or the ethics of *deep ecology*, is also morally varied.[70] Biocentrism, sentientism, and ecocentrism may

---

[64] See Attfield, 2018: 10, 12, 22–23 for the basic divide between anthropocentrism and attributing inherent worth to the environment. See also Schmitt, 1996: 238 (describing them as two distinct cognitive prisms through which to view environmental laws of war). For a summary of the three ways of grounding environmental values, see Singer, 2011: chap. 10; 2000: 86–102.

[65] De-Shalit, 1995; Nolt, 2016: chap. 29. On future generations, see also Attfield, 2018: chap. 3; McMahan, 2020; Singer, 2000: 90–94; 2011: 269–74.

[66] Attfield, 2018: 48–55.

[67] 'Sentientism' grounds ecological protection in the instrumental value of the natural environment for living individuals – human and non-humans alike – who possess the capacity to experience pleasure and pain; Singer, 1974; 1977.

[68] Attfield, 2018: 55; 2005, 85–92. [69] Regan, 1986.

[70] Callicott, 1987; 2015; Hiller, 2016: 203; Leopold, 1980. For a summary of 'deep ecology', see Singer, 2011: 266–88; 2000: 86–102.

or may not be egalitarian in the sense of attributing equal moral value to all living things (biocentric egalitarianism) or even, beyond living things, to natural objects and ecosystems, adding to the multifariousness of perspectives.[71]

For all the theoretical diversity and moral pluralism within environmental ethics and JWT, the duty to protect the natural environment during wartime is the subject of an overlapping consensus on which moral theories are likely to converge, though they will differ in their reasoning and in the extent of protection they afford (e.g. the cross-cutting conclusion that military use of herbicides is wrong).[72] One very basic example of this is the fundamental question of establishing the moral and legal status of the natural environment *in bello*.

1.3 Environmental Non-combatant Immunity

Drucker's early suggestion of extending non-combatant immunity to the environment rests on nature's unquestionably great value, inherently and/or for the well-being of humankind, establishing a moral reason to preserve it. Consequently, Drucker argues, the same arguments that support wartime civilian immunity and the protection of cultural artifacts apply to the environment, to wit: nature is non-threatening (echoing Walzer's explanation of civilian immunity), nor is it in the business of war;[73] it did not choose to be involved; moreover, it provides sustenance and nurture, rendering it akin to medical and religious personnel.[74]

Affording full-fledged non-combatant immunity to the environment, with all the rights that designation implies, is, however, difficult to maintain. One problem with this approach, Michael Deiderich points out, 'is that wars are fought largely in the natural environment, and that a commander would not be expected to sacrifice a soldier to save a tree'.[75] Another concern raised by Hedahl et al. is that wartime civilians have absolute rights against direct attack and military use:

> It would appear to strain credulity to believe that the environment has a right against ever being used as a means to an end. One should not be forced to conclude that digging trenches and thereby using the environment as a means

---

[71] Singer, 2011: 279, 281–82, does not attribute meaningful interests to plants or equal interests to all living things.
[72] Appealing to a wide audience that might value the environment for different moral reasons, Woods, 2007: 24, adopts Reichberg and Syse's 'value agnosticism' regarding these divides.
[73] Walzer, 1977: 144–45.   [74] Drucker, 1989: 136–37, 146–47; see also Woods, 2007: 23.
[75] Deiderich, 1992: 156–57; see also Woods, 2007: 25.

would be wrong, even though using a competent adult who is not involved in hostilities in a similar way might well be.[76]

Notwithstanding, Drucker's basic reasoning is compelling because it encompasses all perspectives and attempts to avoid radical conclusions. Although environmental noncombatant immunity is fully sustainable only on the basis of a deontological morality that attributes inherent worth to the environment, it is, more modestly, analogous to the protection accorded by existing IHL – anthropocentric–utilitarian 'humanitarian' law – to works of art and other cultural assets.[77]

Rejecting the analysis of nature as a genuine 'non-combatant', Hedahl et al. point out that the environment is nonetheless not a combatant, thereby retaining a prima facie presumption against violent attack. Reminding us that the moral default, even in wartime, is against the use of force, the authors argue more plausibly that military violence against nature should require robust justification. They propose that 'impacts to the environment must be appropriately considered in any double-effect calculation', emphasizing their significance in determining proportionality *in bello*.[78]

One advantageous feature of this last proposal to incorporate nature in the proportionality calculus is that it represents a moment of union between conflicting perspectives on human–nature relations. The aforementioned debate within environmental ethics revolves around whether to approach the natural environment as having intrinsic or merely instrumental value for human beings, though, to the extent that we are part of nature, this may be something of a false dichotomy.[79] The environmentally devastating effects of the Russian war in Ukraine, for example, indicate that much of what is bad for nature is harmful to human beings as well. Looking to include animals in the ethics of war, considering the harmful impact on animals within its proportionality calculations, Milburn and Van Goozen point out a similar overlap: 'the JWT requirement of discrimination already rules out many of the forms of warfare that are most impactful on animals. For example, as chemical and nuclear warfare or booby traps are likely to devastate humans as well as animals, JWT already rules these out as indiscriminate.'[80]

In the case in hand, a human-centred approach (anthropocentrism) as well as various non-anthropocentric approaches to environmental ethics (notably biocentrism and ecocentrism) would endorse attributing weighty consideration to environmental damage within wartime proportionality, but the

---

[76] Hedahl et al., 2017: 437.   [77] Drucker, 1989: 139–40, 149–50.
[78] Hedahl et al., 2017: 437.
[79] Johnston, 2016: 3; Reichberg and Syse, 2000: 455–56, similarly regard this division as a 'false dilemma'.
[80] Milburn and Van Goozen, 2023: 436.

former would not endorse the less tenable proposal to equate the status of nature with the absoluteness attached to civilian human rights. Accommodating a range of ethical perspectives – anthropocentric/non-anthropocentric – identifies points of overlapping consensus that enable wide agreement on realistically sustainable advances in protecting the environment at war.

The traditionalist versus revisionist divide within the ethics of war suggests similar benefits of value agnosticism and attaining overlapping consensus between different world-views on environmental protection. Drucker argued for environmental noncombatant immunity because the environment is non-threatening, echoing Walzer's explanation of civilian immunity.[81] Considering the revisionist perspective adds an extra layer of wartime environmental protection to the Walzerian reasoning that regards those who are non-threatening as immune from attack. Revisionist philosophers of war notoriously reject the traditional distinction between threatening combatants and (ostensibly) non-threatening civilians, arguing that the correct criterion of liability to attack in war is not posing a direct threat but rather being morally responsible for an objectively unjustified, wrongful threat.[82] Needless to say, nature is not responsible for wartime injustice any more than it poses a threat, nor is it an agent capable of full moral standing. The environment is innocent in the deep moral sense, and not to blame for war.[83] Moreover, the necessarily continuous range of potential duties towards the environment – before, during, and after armed conflict – should come naturally to revisionist philosophers of war, who reject 'the idea that a different morality comes into effect in conditions of war'.[84] The revisionist 'reductivist' approach to war, which 'treats warfare as morally continuous with all other activities', accords with the realities of protecting the natural environment over time.[85]

Incorporating the revised criterion of liability serves once again to strengthen our presumption against aggression towards entities that are not combatants, but not the far-reaching proposition that would grant the environment full non-combatant status and immunities, on a par with human rights. A morality of war

---

[81] Drucker, 1989: 146; Walzer, 1977: 144–45.
[82] McMahan, 2004: 722–23; 2009: 32–38, 204–5.
[83] Drucker, 1989: 145; McMahan 2009: 9–12.   [84] McMahan, 2012.
[85] Parry, 2015: sec. 2.1; cf. Meron, 1996: 353: 'to be effective, protection of the environment must be continuous and ongoing. It cannot be contingent upon whether there is a state of peace, international war or civil war.' A continuum of duties to protect the natural environment, *para bellum, ad bellum, in bello, post bellum*, is also suggested by Woods, 2007, Drucker, 1989, and Hedahl et al., 2017. On reductivism in revisionist morality of war, as opposed to traditional JWT, see Lazar, 2017: 40–41.

that describes itself as 'individualist' might be hard-pressed to stretch much further away from humanitarianism.[86]

Both theories of the just war are complemented by acknowledging that civilian immunity rests on a basic principle of just combat that proscribes attacking the defenceless.[87] This justification for civilian immunity is particularly applicable to the environment, which is patently defenceless and vulnerable, as are its individual non-human inhabitants.[88] The vulnerability-based justification for protecting sentient beings in wartime crosses animal rights and environmental ethics, with both traditional JWT and revisionism lending the argument greater credence. Maintaining consensus with anthropocentrism, in both environmental and military ethics, reminds us to weigh the welfare of nature and its non-human inhabitants against military goals and human life, and to avoid untenable wartime conclusions that would result from attributing equality to all life forms or absolute non-combatant immunity to the environment.

1.4 Concluding Remarks

The conduct of hostilities is very bad for nature, yet relatively little attention has been focused on environmental military ethics within the voluminous writing by just war theorists and revisionist philosophers of war. Lawyers have done better.

Taking our first steps towards an environmental ethic of war suggests that the strongest moments of moral truth – at least its minimal core content – are present at those points of convergence and consensus between all perspectives. Points of agreement between conflicting ethical camps, notably utilitarianism and Kantian moral philosophies, anthropocentric and non-anthropocentric environmental ethics, and traditional and revisionist moralities of war, indicate moments of moral truth. Unless all our normative thinking is askew, it is unlikely that all approaches would be wrong on a particular issue. When in uncharted moral territory, this is probably the most solid ground from which to set out.

On a practical note, despite contemporary public attention on environmental deterioration (Greta Thunberg notwithstanding), the idea of protecting nature during wartime does not come easily. At least at first blush, wartime concern for

---

[86] Lazar, 2017: 40: 'They think that only individuals act in war, not collectives (they are descriptive individualists), and they think that only individuals matter in war (they are evaluative individualists).' My understanding of the latter is 'only individual humans matter in war'. It would not be inconceivable for the revisionist theory of just war to extend such value to individual creatures of different species, but this does not seem to be the case at present.
[87] Lazar, 2010; Meisels, 2012; 2017: 31–48; Shue, 1978: 125, 129; 2008: 87–111.
[88] Milburn and Van Goozen, 2021.

human life and well-being appears far too pressing to allow for consideration of wildlife, far less to protect it at the expense of human beings.[89] It is difficult enough to persuade warring parties to respect the lives of enemy civilians at the expense of their own military advantage, let alone value a species of animal or their natural habitats.[90]

Accommodating different perspectives and focusing on points of consensus should prevent unrealistic extremes from either environmentalism or militarism and help avoid conclusions that are well-argued and morally attractive in theory (on paper) but are realistically impractical. Coming at this from environmental ethics or deep moral philosophy risks over-zealous environmentalism, placing unduly demanding restrictions on war-making, verging on pacifism, as well as on its individual participants, whose lives are already at risk. At the other end of the equation, militarism, pure anthropocentrism, or *raison d'état* alone will likely overemphasize 'necessity' and downplay environmental harms in relation to immediate military advantage.

The status of the environment in wartime is a clear case study for overlapping consensus: affording absolute civilian immunity to the natural environment is unjustified from a humanist perspective, and untenable from a military standpoint; but the lesser analogy with cultural artifacts can be supported by a full host of relevant moral theories. Referring to existing law as a benchmark, this equilibrium is well reflected in the Red Cross's articulation of the aforementioned relevant legal rules in Protocol I: 'Except in rare cases when it has become a military objective, it is against the law to attack the natural environment.'[91]

2 Environmental Just Wars: *Jus ad Bellum* and the Natural Environment

War is bad for the environment. As discussed in Section 1, contemporary ecological concerns pose significant challenges to *jus in bello*, or military ethics.[92] Nevertheless, despite growing awareness of environmental issues, just war theorists and moral philosophers of war have paid insufficient attention to the military's carbon footprint, notwithstanding notable exceptions reviewed in the previous section.[93] The law and legal scholars have paid more attention to protecting nature during armed conflict. In this area, the law, by virtue of necessity, precedes moral scholarship and may serve to advance it. But, because

---

[89] Drucker, 1989: 135, 148; Roberts, 2000: 48; Schmitt, 1996: 249; 1997: 59.
[90] Deiderich, 1992: 156–58; Hedahl et al., 2017: 431; Woods, 2007: 25.   [91] ICRC, 2019.
[92] Hedahl et al., 2017: 432–36.
[93] Especially: Drucker, 1989; Estève, 2020; Hedahl et al., 2017; Johnston, 2015; Milburn and Van Goozen, 2021; Reichberg and Syse, 2000; Woods, 2007.

the International Law of Armed Conflict focuses primarily on the rules of engagement regulating the conduct of hostilities, issues concerning environmentally just and unjust wars have received even less normative attention than environmental protection in war.[94]

The current *jus ad bellum* legal regime does not recognize any environmental injuries that fall short of 'armed attack' as just causes for war, and the dangers of legalizing additional occasions for war go without saying. Because of the different nature and functions of morality and law, even the most practical ethics may not translate directly into legal proposals; law must account for a multitude of practicalities that may elude moral philosophers of war.[95] This does not settle the issue at hand or render futile the consideration of future environmental causes for war. As new dangers emerge, ethical deliberation should eventually guide and influence the *jus ad bellum* regime. Ethical reflection on timely concerns should ultimately help inform and shape a legal regime that takes emerging environmental concerns more seriously.

Empirically, the natural environment plays a very significant role in the resort to war. Natural wealth (such as oil) funds and encourages participants in civil wars; greed for the riches of the earth – diamonds, oil, and other natural resources – may partly explain the onset, duration, and ferocity of these wars.[96] Links between climate change and conflicts have been debated within the academic literature, indicating that an increasing number of wars are being driven by environmental destruction, by climate change, and by resource scarcity.[97] As global climate change progresses and areas of the world become uninhabitable, conflicts over living space and scarce natural resources are likely to increase, placing pressure on the current *jus ad bellum* regime.[98]

The following two subsections focus on potential ecological justifications for war as well as on the proportionality of any such recourse to arms on behalf of the environment. Setting out with the presumption against the use of force, Subsection 2.1 considers whether environmental harm can form a new

---

[94] Exceptions to the philosophical neglect of *jus ad bellum* in connection with the environment are: Eckersley, 2007; Hedahl et al., 2017: esp. 432–35; Martin, 2020; Reichberg and Syse, 2000: 460–62; Woods, 2007, 25–30.
[95] Reichberg and Syse, 2000: 450; Waldron, 2010: 88.
[96] Collier and Hoeffler, 2004; Fabre, 2012: 135; Wenar, 2008.
[97] Koubi, 2019; Johnston, 2016. The prospect of future 'resource wars', e.g. over fresh water in the Middle East, is conceivable. Arguably, a very serious failure to collaborate in shared resource management, such as drawing down aquifers or oil reserves, taking far more than one's fair share, might in future amount to a just cause for war. While this potential source of international conflict concerns natural resources (who uses what and how much), it does not necessarily concern harm to the environment, and as such exceeds the scope of this section. For a full discussion of these issues, see Nine, 2022, arguing for a requirement to manage shared resources collaboratively. I am grateful to Avery Kolers for this comment.
[98] Hedahl et al., 2017: 433–35; Martin, 2020.

justification for war, presumably in the context of war's prima facie unjustifiability. Subsection 2.2 asks how the environment figures into the proportionality of war itself (as distinct from the *jus in bello* requirement to minimize collateral damage).[99] Subsection 2.3 asks who the 'right authority' would be to declare war for environmental reasons.

My answers are not definitive. The use of force is clearly justified in response to military aggression, whether against the natural environment or otherwise. Where harm to nature or its inhabitants is not caused by military attack, JWT criteria point in favour of responding via measures short of war. Combating harm to nature by military means always runs a high risk of causing more environmental harm than good. Non-military measures – international pressures, protests, and sanctions – do not require satisfying the *jus ad bellum* proportionality (or 'just authority') requirement, but any resort to arms does require meeting these conditions. Resorting to limited force short of all out war – e.g. pinpointed drone strikes and cyber-attacks – mitigates the risk of disproportionality. Finally, I suggest that resorting to soft power and possibly limited force – less harmful to the environment than full-scale armed conflict – as well as international cooperation, also helps satisfy the 'just authority' condition and serves to indicate 'right intention', deflecting suspicions about the use of force to advance state interests on the pretext of environmental protection.

2.1 Environmental Just Cause

To start with, on all accounts, wars must have a just cause, typically that of resisting aggression (national self-defence). Traditionally, aggression is 'the crime of war'.[100] In the post-World War II era, the prohibition against the use of force among states, as well as the exceptions to it (self-defence and UN Security Council authorization), are well-established within the UN Charter system.[101] Effectively, contemporary international law and JWT now recognize only one just cause for waging war unilaterally: self- or other defence against aggression understood as the occurrence of an armed attack[102] '(with the possible exception of the prevention of large-scale violations of human rights, such as genocide)'.[103] Reichberg and Syse explain:

---

[99] Hedahl et al., 2017: 434–35 on 'proportionality of ends'; Hedahl and Fruh, 2019: 391; Woods, 2007: 26–27 on 'Macro-Proportionality'.

[100] Grotius, 1625/2012: Book II, Chapter I: 'Defense of Person and Property'. Wars are criminal when waged without just cause. Hurka, 2005: 35; Walzer, 1977: 21.

[101] The United Nations Charter, Chapter I, Article 2(4) and Chapter VII, Article 51.

[102] McMahan, 2005: 1; Walzer, 1977: 53–54.   [103] McMahan, 2005: 7.

Since war is prima facie an evil, participation in it requires moral and legal justification. Thus, according to the moral logic of 'just cause', war-making will be deemed rightful or just solely when it arises as a response to grave wrongdoing committed by the other side.[104]

On a revisionist–individualist version of JWT, 'a just cause for war is a wrong that is of a type that can make those responsible for it morally liable to military attack as a means of preventing or rectifying it'.[105] On both versions of JWT – revisionist and traditionalist – as well as international law, the ultimate objective of war is protecting basic human rights, whether via national self-defence or, more reductively, individual self-defence.[106]

Environmental destruction is often part and parcel of an ongoing aggressive attack on a state's sovereignty and its members' basic rights. Russian aggression towards Ukraine supplies ample examples of assaults on the natural environment that also threaten life and liberty.[107] This is aggression *simpliciter*. Airborne incendiary devices launched from the Gaza Strip into Southern Israel between 2018 and 2023 – setting forests and fields alight, wreaking long-term ecological damage – present far lower-intensity cases of contemporary environmental aggression, discussed in Section 4.[108] As no Israelis were killed or injured in these attacks, the level of aggression and the appropriate response remain debatable issues. In hindsight, they pale in comparison with the murderous October 7 invasion. Nonetheless, kites and balloons were military incursions that crossed borders and caused widespread environmental harm on Israeli territory, straightforwardly violating sovereignty and individual rights to personal safety and private property.[109] In both the Israeli and the Ukrainian cases, attacks against land and property, whatever their degree, fit comfortably within traditional JWT; the crime of aggression is not limited to bodily harm or killing.[110]

Suggesting a rich history of attributing significance to environmental impacts within just war deliberations, Hedahl et al. point out that Vitoria included damaging the environment (e.g. by burning vineyards or olive gardens) among the just causes for war,[111] though notably vineyards and olive gardens are human-made. Grotius compared the severity of poisoning the land to poisoning a person, both warranting the right to defend, recover, and punish,

---

[104] Reichberg and Syse, 2000: 461.   [105] McMahan 2005: 1 (abstract).
[106] Lazar, 2017: 41–42.
[107] See e.g. among many reports, Avdoshyn et al., 2019; Rawtani et al., 2022.
[108] Zych, 2019: esp. 76; *Times of Israel*, 2018.
[109] Moodrick-Even Khen, 2019: 336, 329; Stefanini, 2021: 664, 670.
[110] Walzer, 1977: 52, 62.
[111] Hedahl et al., 2017: 430; with reference to Vitoria, 1532/1991: sec. 54, 324, n. 49.

within or between political communities respectively.[112] As with Vitoria, attributing care for the natural environment per se to Hugo Grotius is a bit of a stretch: poisoning the land is a wrong to humans, who will not be able to use the land, rather than a wrong to the land itself. Nonetheless, as 'the father of international law' it is noteworthy that he regarded violence towards land as a *casus belli*.

Setting out with this tradition, it is not unthinkable to argue, as does Robyn Eckersley, that major environmental emergencies with transboundary spillover effects that threaten public safety; for example, 'Chernobyl-style' threats of nuclear explosion, would morally and legally justify military action. This is the strongest and most minimalist argument for ecological intervention because 'incursions of pollution or hazardous substances into the territory of neighboring states are analogous to an "armed attack" with chemical, biological, or nuclear weapons; they enter or threaten to enter the territory of the victim state without its consent and with equally grave consequences.'[113] This first set of cases would count as threats to territorial integrity, rendering an environmental just cause, per se, redundant as justification for war, because just cause could be captured by the right to defend sovereignty.

A second case is where severe ecological harm, or 'ecocide', accompanies grave human rights violations, on a par with genocide or crimes against humanity. Here, Eckersley continues, justifying military action rides on the back of humanitarian intervention – 'eco-humanitarian intervention' – and is subject to all the controversies and challenges surrounding the emerging norm of responsibility to protect, and then some.[114] Legally, there is no such 'eco-humanitarian' basis for war in current international law, and even humanitarian intervention does not yet constitute a clear exception to the prohibition on the use of force.

The most interesting question remains whether environmental concerns could ever constitute a wrong that gives rise to 'just cause', even if a state's territory has not been invaded and where no basic human rights have been directly infringed.[115] Territorial invasions and genocide that involve harm to the natural environment do not stray far from conventional justifications for war. Responding to environmental harms that do not involve territorial incursion or violation of human rights would rest entirely on ecological grounds.[116]

---

[112] Hedahl et al., 2017: 430; Grotius, 1625/2012: Book II, Chapter I.
[113] Eckersley, 2007: 295–301.   [114] Eckersley, 2007: 301–4.
[115] See McMahan, 2020: 230–32, for a futuristic example of 'climate war' against a state that refused to cooperate with international policies preventing climate change.
[116] Ecological grounds for war might also include obligations to future people, not well captured by familiar rights-based analyses. See McMahan, 2020: esp. 230–32, on the 'non-identity problem'.

Eckersley considers extending the idea of responsibility to protect (R2P) to non-human species and biodiversity, that is, military intervention to prevent 'ecocide' or 'crimes against nature' in themselves, even where consequences are confined to the culprit state causing harm to its own environment. If we view relations between humans and nature in trustor–trustee, or custodianship, terms, it follows that the destruction of species and ecosystems is a dereliction of duty.[117] On this account, deliberate and wilful acts that cause grave environmental damage (e.g. Iraq setting fire to Kuwait's oil fields) or extermination of species (e.g. the threat of poachers annihilating mountain gorillas) might then be regarded as war crimes in the first instance, or comparable to conscience-shocking 'crimes against humanity' in the second, possibly triggering 'just cause' for international military intervention (subject to the remaining just war requirements).[118]

For present purposes, I set aside the question of justifying military action solely on behalf of other species or nature per se without resorting to any human interests. Establishing a purely ecological just cause for war would require settling the most basic divides within environmental ethics – anthropocentric versus non-anthropocentric – in all its variety.[119] Justifying intervention to protect a local environment – its ecosystems, species, and habitats – as being on a par with the ideal of humanitarian intervention to protect human life might require a doctrine of conditional sovereignty whereby the right against interference is contingent upon meeting minimal environmental moral standards.[120] Legally, such a basis for war does not even remotely exist in international law. Military rescue of non-human species, extending R2P to biological diversity, is unlikely and doubtfully desirable, considering the high costs of war. Moreover, in most real-world cases, the extreme type of environmental harm that could even potentially justify war would likely be bad for humans as well, at least indirectly, and exceed national boundaries.[121]

---

[117] Reichberg and Syse, 2000: 457–58 (following Aquinas) on 'stewardship'. Eckersley, 2007: 310, attributes this trusteeship approach to contemporary treaty law.

[118] Eckersley, 2007: 293, 296, 305, esp. 310–11. On the possibility that large-scale harm to animals or to animal species could constitute a just cause and the difficulty in fulfilling the other JWT requirements in such cases, see Milburn and Van Goozen, 2023: 429–31, 'War for Animals'; 431–33, 'War to Save Biodiversity'. Regarding climate change, see also Martin, 2020: esp. 378–83 on analogies with humanitarian intervention and R2P.

[119] I restate the 'value agnosticism' on environmental ethics and attaining 'overlapping consensus' on environmental protection in wartime, introduced by Reichberg and Syse, 2000: 452–53, and adopted by Woods, 2007: 24, as it is here, appealing to a wide audience.

[120] Compare Teson, 1995, 2001, 2006, on humanitarian intervention.

[121] This does not assume complete harmony of interests between human beings and nature. It is easy to envision cases of annihilation of species, harm to organisms, natural habitats, etc., even 'ecocide' that does not affect humans in any considerable way. Given, however, that 'war is hell', as General Sherman asserted and Walzer, 1977: 32, reminds us, I do not entertain the

Discussing World Heritage Sites that lie within the territorial boundaries of sovereign states, Cecile Fabre supplies a timely example recalling the 2019 fires in the Amazon rainforest.

> These are regular occurrences, which inflict untold damage on homes, animal species, and the planet's ecosystems. Anger at what many regard as the Brazilian authorities' unconscionably reckless approach to deforestation has focused on its environmental impact for present and future generations.[122]

In such cases, Fabre suggests, outsiders have a claim to the preservation and, if necessary, restoration of 'humankind's common heritage'.[123] Following UNESCO's World Heritage List, these include not only universally valuable man-made landmarks, such as Notre Dame de Paris, but also natural landscapes, rivers, mountains, and lakes, like the Smokey Mountains in the US or Lake Baikal in Russia, noting that some landmarks are valuable not only as heritage but also for instrumental reasons.[124]

The Amazon rainforest is (arguably) said to produce 20 per cent of the Earth's atmospheric oxygen. Clearly, beyond UNESCO's World Heritage List well-noted by Fabre, the Amazon is a global systematic resource – 'global public commons' – required for the balance of the earth's systems. Its burning caused severe harm to the ecosystem, vital to the planet, and warrants its protection. Consequently, the fires became something of an international crisis, with Brazil's lax policy prompting the aforementioned anger of, and fierce response from, world leaders (memorably, French President Emmanuel Macron) culminating in a threat by G7 countries to withdraw from trade negotiations with Brazil.

In response, President Jair Bolsonaro accused the G7 leaders of intervening in Brazil's internal affairs. Despite repeated pleas from the international community and non-governmental organizations, Brazil refused to revise its environmental policies, with possible dire ramifications in terms of deforestation and climate change. This is of course just one example of the international

---

possibility of waging war to save 'a tree, a forest, or even an ecosystem' (Hedahl et al., 2017: 431), though I am aware that others might, e.g. Eckersley, 2007. I assume there are enough cases of overlapping environmental concerns for humans and the non-human world to challenge existing JWT conceptions of just cause, without considering resort to arms for nature's own sake.

[122] Fabre, 2021: 20.

[123] Fabre, 2021: 20–21 on the Amazon. By 'heritage', she has in mind 'that which we inherit from our ancestors, which we value here and now and which we seek to transmit to our successors for reasons which have nothing to do with its extractive value' (17). On common heritage and humankind's common concern, see also Eckersley, 2007: 307–10.

[124] Fabre, 2021: 19.

community's persistent failure to guarantee compliance on environmental issues (e.g. climate change mitigation, ecological protection, biodiversity conservation, etc.).[125]

Whether or not one accepts the argument for 'Humankind's Common Heritage' in toto, the example of wildfires in the Brazilian Amazon rainforest and resultant deforestation presents a uniquely good case study for reflecting on the permissibility of resorting to force to avert grave ecological destruction, when all else has failed.[126]

In keeping with the G7 threat, Fabre maintains that the protection of outsiders' interests in such sites of ecological or cultural significance is an *enforceable* duty of justice, suggesting the appropriateness of economic sanctions, expulsion from international organizations, reduction in foreign aid, and so on, in cases like this one.[127] Could extreme dereliction of duty to maintain vital ecological sites also justify force as a last resort?

Not unrelated to the notion of common heritage or global resources (albeit in regard to *jus in bello*), Reichberg and Syse allude to the natural law tradition whereby all property is originally and ultimately common to humankind, while private property is fully justified as expedient.

> Thus, the destruction of, say, farmland, rain forests, or oil resources constitutes not only a violation of the property rights of those who live in or own that area now; it is also a way of destroying property which in a sense is common to all of mankind, including future generations … This entails a moral prohibition against large-scale devastation of territory, even within one's own national jurisdiction.[128]

Considering the gravity of contemporary environmental concerns, the idea of an ecological just cause arising from such devastation even in one's own territory, or of resisting 'environmental aggression', is far from fanciful. In the Amazonian case and most others, environmental destruction is manifestly bad for human beings, not only nature per se – at least in the long run – perhaps

---

[125] Martin, 2020, on present and predictable failure to mobilize international compliance with climate change obligations; esp. regarding deforestation of the Amazon and President Bolsonaro's behaviour: 334 n. 10, 336–37, 346, 365, 370, 403.

[126] In the case in hand Fabre, 2021: 20–21, reminds us: 'the Central Amazon Conservation Complex, … located in seven states, is protected by the World Heritage at the bar of two of UNESCO's 10 criteria for inclusion: it represents "significant on-going ecological and biological processes in the evolution and development of terrestrial, freshwater, coastal and marine ecosystems and communities of plants and animals" (criterion ix); it contains "the most important and significant natural habitats for in-situ conservation of biological diversity, including those containing threatened species of outstanding universal value from the point of view of science or conservation" (criterion x).'

[127] Fabre, 2021: 22.

[128] Reichberg and Syse, 2000: 463, regarding the requirement of discrimination.

violating our common property or resources, as well as harmful to animals and inanimate components of nature. Climate change is a case in point.

Appealing to the just war framework, Marcus Hedahl and Kyle Fruh suggest that carbon-emitting activities perpetuating global warming constitute aggression towards the most vulnerable to its effects, to wit, low-lying lands such as Tuvalu, which will soon face existential threat as a result.[129] 'In perpetrating climate change, we are, in fact, waging war against the most vulnerable.'[130] Climate change, they argue, is an unjust war justifying self-defence on behalf of the injured party.[131] Subsequently, they defend retaliation by these nations via geoengineering, specifically solar radiation management (SRM), which is equally construed as an act of war but justified in these cases.[132] Ultimately, they concede their argument also suggests that in principle 'In the right circumstances, low-lying nations *would* possess the normative authority to engage in kinetic attacks on GHG-producing facilities.'[133]

The threat to be averted notwithstanding, establishing a 'green just cause', even from a purely anthropocentric stance, would not at present fit easily with any known version of JWT, and would require considerable (perhaps desirable) adjustment of existing tenets in either its traditional or its revisionist account, as well as international law. As Hedahl and Fruh recognize, paradigmatic aggression consists in the intentional and deliberate use of force by an identifiable party against territorial integrity or political sovereignty.[134] Causing environmental damage does not necessarily entail the use of military means of the type that would ordinarily generate just cause for war in response to an armed attack. In the Brazilian example, 'just cause' would be distinct from self-defence on both traditionalist and revisionist versions of JWT because outsiders' basic rights are not necessarily undermined or impaired by failure to preserve a site such as the Amazon – at least not directly or immediately – nor was any nation-state invaded by an act constituting outright 'aggression' in any traditional or legal sense.[135]

All the same, bearing in mind increasing anthropogenic destruction and climate change, it is not impossible to envision continuous and future transgression that would violate the human right to a safe environment, both individually and communally, hampering another nation's ability to 'determine their own levels of environmental quality' as well as individual health and well-being.[136]

---

[129] Hedahl and Fruh, 2019: 378–79.   [130] Hedahl and Fruh, 2019: 378.
[131] Hedahl and Fruh, 2019: 378, 380, 395–96, and *passim*.   [132] Hedahl and Fruh, 2019.
[133] Hedahl and Fruh, 2019: 396.   [134] Hedahl and Fruh, 2019: 379, 386.
[135] Compare Fabre, 2021: 18.
[136] Compare Eckersley, 2007: 300, interpretation of 'territorial integrity or political independence' in Article 2(4) of the UN Charter. Hedahl and Fruh, 2019, similarly reinterpret aggression and the right to self-defence within JWT regarding climate change. On the global injustice and

This might indeed constitute 'aggression' even if no border is crossed, potentially justifying recourse to force in response if and when all else fails. In revisionist terms, grave ecological negligence or harm to the non-human world could constitute a wrong of sufficient severity to render responsible individuals in the perpetrator state liable to defensive attack, if attacking them could correct, or considerably mitigate, the environmental wrong in question.[137]

It is difficult to specify exhaustively the wide variety of possibilities that might potentially trigger a future 'just cause'. As global environmental degradation continues to unfold, urgency will have a bearing on these issues. Once again, the easiest cases are those in which harm to nature involves conventional invasion of territory, as with the environmental damage due to the war in Ukraine, or inflammatory airborne devices entering Israel. Next, following Eckersley, emitting harmful substances directly into another state is arguably analogous to territorial invasion.[138] Large emissions of greenhouse gases, however, are unfortunately still the norm, and therefore it would be very difficult for anything resembling the present understanding to justify an exceptional resort to force, despite the far-reaching and long-term consequences of rising temperatures.[139] Clear breaches of existing international law (e.g. blowing up Antarctica), on the other hand, would be better candidates for intervention. The weakest cases for intervention, straying furthest from existing law, are those of states destroying only their local environment, where the devastation is entirely contained within their own national jurisdiction, though arguably any environmental harm affects us all at least indirectly and destroys property common to mankind, including future generations.[140]

Acknowledging a non-comprehensive range stretching from old-fashioned violation of sovereignty at one end, and local harm to one's own territory or national resources at the other, Bolsonaro's Brazil supplied a timely example of a state destroying its own environment and at the same time damaging its population and the world at large. Nonetheless, where no actual or imminent armed attack is present, justifying war to combat environmental harm is unlikely to fulfil the *jus ad bellum* principle of proportionality.

---

human rights violations involved in climate change and the individual right to resist, see Caney, 2015: esp. 52, 55, 59, 69.

[137] Compare McMahan, 2005.   [138] Eckersley, 2007: 295–301.
[139] Compare Hedahl and Fruh, 2019: 396.
[140] Compare Eckersley, 2007: 307–10; Fabre, 2021; Reichberg and Syse, 2000: 463. On obligations towards future generations, see again: De-Shalit, 1995; Nolt, 2016: chap. 29. On future generations, see also Attfield, 2018: chap. 3; McMahan, 2020, on the non-identity problem; Singer, 2000: 90–94; 2011: 269–74.

2.2 What Is a Proportionate Response?

Even if 'just cause' could be adjusted to accommodate non-military environmental wrongs, the further *ad bellum* criterion of proportionality would still be difficult to satisfy in cases of purely ecological harm. As for armed environmental aggression, military attacks on the environment would count as a threat to territorial integrity (which, along with political independence, constitutes sovereignty). Such cases would not require an environmental just cause per se, because they could be captured by the right to defend sovereignty, responding to 'armed attack'. Even so, military response may harm the environment to an extent that dwarfs its benefit. In keeping with proportionality, what unilateral military measures, if any, might states employ to fend off environmental harm?

The relevant international legal documents – the UN Charter[141] and UN Security Council Resolutions – do not contain positive references to proportionality *ad bellum* as a limitation on self-defence in response to an armed attack. Nevertheless, such a restriction is recognized as part of customary international law.[142] Originally derived from the 1837 *Caroline* incident,[143] and reinforced more recently by several opinions of the International Court of Justice (ICJ),[144] it is widely acknowledged that a military operation should not exceed the goal of restoring the status quo that predated the armed attack to which it is responding – self-defence should not be retaliatory or punitive and reprisals are generally agreed to be unlawful – though this does not tell us much about the legitimate extent of response.[145]

As opposed to proportionality *in bello* regulated by International Humanitarian Law, *ad bellum* proportionality applies to the legitimacy of the forceful action in total, rather than its specific tactics.[146] It throws a wide net rather than focusing narrowly on collateral damage to civilians, applying instead to the general overall level of devastation anticipated as a result of the proposed military action. This would include the harm of violating territorial integrity, damage to infrastructure, effects on third parties, and so on,[147] and presumably all damage to the natural environment. Nonetheless, the indeterminacies of this requirement far exceed its

---

[141] Charter of the United Nations, Chapter VII, Article 51.
[142] Gardam, 1993: 391–413; 2004: 11–12; 2005: 3–6; Grey, 2008: 148–50, and his accompanying footnotes 147 and 150.
[143] Grey, 2008: 148–49; Gardam, 2005: 3.
[144] Grey, 2008: 149–50, with reference to: *Military and Para-Military Activities in and Against Nicaragua*, ICJ Reps. (1986), p. 14, Para. 194; *Oil Platforms Case* (Iran v. United States), ICJ Reps. (2003), p. 161, Para. 43; *Armed Activities on the Territory of the Congo* (Democratic Republic of Congo v. Uganda), ICJ Reps. (2005), p. 168, Para. 147; *ICJ: The Legality of the Threat or Use of Nuclear Weapons*, ICJ Reps. (1996), p. 226. Para. 141, 143.
[145] Gardam, 2005: 7, 13–24; Grey, 2008: 150–51. [146] Lee, 2012: 214.
[147] Gardam, 2005: 5.

discernable limits; and the specific content of any legal *ad bellum* proportionality test remains extremely vague and controversial, as it does within the JWT that underlies it.

As for the just war tradition, all versions include an *ad bellum* proportionality condition that applies to the war as a whole, requiring that its destructiveness must not be excessive in relation to the relevant good it will achieve.[148] This was Vitoria's understanding, echoed in countless contemporary discussions of proportionality.[149] Thomas Hurka explains that *ad bellum* proportionality requires balancing the good that the war is designed to bring about – the wrong it is intended to avert – against the harm that the war causes.[150] It involves weighing the costs and benefits of war overall, though how exactly these are to be estimated or compared remains very vague.[151]

What seems clear and pertinent is that proportionality in *jus ad bellum* is inevitably tied to just cause: an aggressive war cannot have any relevant benefits to balance against the harm it inflicts. Without just cause, there are no sufficient harms that warrant armed resistance. Only a war fought for a good cause, typically wars of self-defence, can pass the *ad bellum* proportionality test.[152] When wars are fought for the right reasons, the benefits side of the proportionality calculus includes their initial just cause – resisting aggression.

Just war theory also acknowledges several legitimate 'conditional' goals that the military is entitled to pursue, such as disarming a threatening enemy and deterring further aggression. Additional wartime goals are conditional in that they would not in themselves justify the resort to war. Nonetheless, when they accompany an initially sufficient just cause for war, specifically self-defence, these additional goals count as potential benefits that weigh against the harms of the war and contribute to its proportionality.[153]

This invariable link between justice of cause and proportionality comes to the fore when considering a new *casus belli*, namely environmental harm. First, the distinction between 'sufficient' and 'contributing' (conditional) just causes is particularly pertinent to the environmental benefits of war and their contribution to its proportionality calculations. While it may not be permissible at present to fight wars for purely environmental reasons, morally valuable ends such as

---

[148] Hurka, 2005: 35.
[149] Lee, 2012: 85–86 cites Vitoria's understanding of (*in bello*) proportionality as 'the obligation to see that greater evils do not arise out of the war than the war would avert'; Vitoria, 1532/1991: esp. 303–8, 315. See also McMahan, 2009: 18. Kasher, 2009: 43–75, 53, describes the balance in very similar terms, referring to it as 'Macro-Proportionality'; Hedahl and Fruh, 2019: 391 on 'wide proportionality'; Rodin, 2003: 114.
[150] Hurka, 2005: 38–66 (relevant goods and evils).
[151] Forge, 2009: 26, 28; Lee, 2012: 85–93, esp. 214.   [152] Lee, 2012: 214; Hurka, 2005: 37.
[153] Hurka, 2005: 41; McMahan and Mckin, 1993: 512–13.

promoting environmental justice might serve to add legitimacy to a war that already has a lawful just cause. Recognizing a 'conditional' environmental goal would increase the benefits side of proportionality calculations, presumably licensing greater use of force or allowing more destruction/harms, because of the 'additional' justice.

On the other hand, ecological justifications for war pose a special type of complication for the proportionality calculus. While environmental concerns may broaden the scope of just cause, the inevitable devastation caused by warfare makes proportionality more difficult to satisfy. Irrespective of whether the ecological harm was inflicted via armed attack or not, warfare undertaken for environmental protection will foreseeably cause further damage to the natural environment, which may well outweigh its gains.[154] Moreover, full-scale military responses to non-military harm, or even to armed attacks that are largely non-lethal to humans, would likely be viewed as excessive by both public and legal opinion.

One practical way to meet these challenges is by resorting to limited belligerency in response to environmental wrongs without incurring the extent of devastation that would outweigh the benefits of military action. This includes tactics covered by *jus ad vim* – the just use of force short of war – that fall below the breadth and intensity of traditional warfare, notably pinpointed air strikes with drones as well as non-kinetic (unarmed) tactics.[155]

Like most contemporary just war thinking, the discussion of *jus ad vim* begins with Michael Walzer's *Just and Unjust Wars*, specifically with the preface to its fourth edition. There, Walzer distinguishes traditional *jus ad bellum,* governing the resort to actual war (full-scale attacks, invasions), from the moral principles that govern the resort to force short of war, dubbed *jus ad vim*. As Walzer explains, the measures governed by *jus ad vim* involve the use (or threat) of force – embargos or the enforcement of no-fly zones, limited airstrikes with drones, etc. – and consequently count as acts of war under international law. Nonetheless, it is common sense to recognize that they are very different from war.[156]

---

[154] Hedahl et al., 2017: 429, 433–35; Woods, 2007: 28.

[155] Walzer, 2006a: xv–xvii. On non-kinetic tactics, see Gross and Meisels, 2017. Betz, 2019: esp. 238–41, relies on Gross and Meisels' introduction to suggest both *jus ad vim* and soft war to combat climate change offenders; however, his only scenario for applying these measures is a highly hypothetical 'world of near-universal compliance with abatement obligations and would be directed at the few remaining environmental wrongdoers' (241) rendering these tactics ultimately unjustified regarding environmental harms in the contemporary real world.

[156] Walzer, 2006a: xvi, *jus ad vim*. This framework of '*jus ad vim*' as an in-between space between war and law enforcement is developed by Brunstetter and Braun, 2013.

Full-scale conflict always involves grave risks and hazards, unpredictable and all too often catastrophic consequences, and the full-fledged 'hellishness of war' described throughout *Just and Unjust Wars* and enhanced if we count non-human casualties alongside harm to the natural surroundings. Bearing in mind the link between just cause and proportionality as well as the high environmental costs of military action, resorting to full-scale war to fend off ecological hazards, even if they give rise to 'just cause', is unlikely to satisfy the *ad bellum* proportionality requirement to cause more benefit than harm.[157]

By contrast, *jus ad vim* measures are limited in their scope and intensity, requiring far less force and harm to their surroundings, as well as less risk to their perpetrators. This is certainly the case with embargos and no-fly zones.[158] As for drones, as Laurie Johnston points out, they 'have less of a carbon footprint because they are less resource intensive. They use less fuel than manned aircraft.'[159] Moreover, echoing McMahan's criterion of liability, Adam Betz points out in connection with targeted killing, 'A major advantage of these tactics ... is the fact that they can be more readily directed at liable parties'.[160]

Opposing any relaxation of the prohibition on the use of force to accommodate 'atmospheric intervention' against egregious climate change offenders (e.g. Brazil), Martin nonetheless recognizes that the type of force potentially relevant in such cases would be 'limited surgical strikes against precisely the infrastructure related to the noncompliant conduct ... pertinent historical examples would be the Israeli surgical air strikes against the Iraqi nuclear facility at Osirak in 1981, or again its strike against the Syrian nuclear facility in 2007.'[161]

One risk with air strikes is that they could degenerate into all out international armed conflict.[162] A further disadvantage concerns the *jus in bello* core principle of distinction and civilian immunity. As opposed to targeting nuclear munition plants:

> the entire premise of atmospheric intervention is that the use of force would be targeted at infrastructure or facilities directly related to the contribution of GHGs [greenhouse gases], it is highly unlikely that such targets could be legitimately characterized as anything other than civilian objects.[163]

---

[157] Milburn and Van Goozen, 2023: 433, recommend applying Brunstetter and Braun's, 2013, *jus ad vim* framework to the protection of animals and animal species, such as 'the war on poaching', unlikely to satisfy the JWT requirement of last resort, noting targeted drone strikes (e.g. against poachers) 'outside of war traditionally understood'.
[158] Walzer, 2006a: xvi.   [159] Johnston, 2016: 2.   [160] Betz, 2019: 241.
[161] Martin, 2020: 404.   [162] Martin, 2020: 404.   [163] Martin, 2020: 409–10.

Legally, as well as in traditional JWT, air strikes may be deployed only against military targets. When dealing with environmental harms, as in the Amazon example, aiming at combatants may not be relevant. Hedahl and Fruh entertain the possibility of low-lying nations justifiably launching tactical kinetic attacks at GHG-emitting facilities, if this could facilitate their battle against climate change.[164] A revisionist account of the ethics of war might conceivably justify targeting culpable civilians responsible for grave environmental negligence, if killing them (or destroying related civilian infrastructure) were likely to halt, or seriously diminish, ongoing ecological harm.[165] More palatable to traditionalists and lawyers, alternative measures short of war also include non-kinetic, 'soft war' tactics – 'softer' alternatives to kinetic power, such as media and propaganda warfare, economic restrictions, and even cyber-attacks – to halt or repel environmental harms without targeting non-combatants and civilian objects or falling foul of any proportionality requirement.[166]

Tactics covered by *jus ad vim* are, by definition, forceful measures albeit short of large-scale war, often involving kinetic force, notably the use of drones for targeted killing or pinpointed attacks on relevant facilities. Legally, there is no gradation in the use of force or 'armed conflict'. Consequently, as Walzer notes, *jus ad vim* acts are clearly governed by international laws of war and appropriate for combatting military targets and objectives.[167] The concept of soft war, by contrast, encompasses non-kinetic tactics – e.g. economic and media/information warfare, individual boycotts, and 'lawfare' – that do not involve a resort to arms and therefore, apart from intense cyber-attacks, mostly do not count legally as acts of war at all.[168] Consequently, directing these tactics at non-compliant civilians does not violate non-combatant immunity, on any account of JWT or international law. Pinpointed strikes against *military* targets respect civilian immunity; measures short of attack are not bound by its requirements.[169]

---

[164] Hedahl and Fruh, 2019: 396. [165] Compare McMahan, 2005.
[166] See Gross and Meisels, 2017. Similarly, recall in connection with the Amazon rainforest Fabre, 2021: 22, who notes economic sanctions, expulsion from international organizations, and reduction in foreign aid as appropriate responses.
[167] Morally speaking (not legally) they fall outside the remit of *jus ad bellum*, Walzer suggests, and require a separate and somewhat more permissive, ethical framework. Walzer, 2006a: xv–xvi.
[168] One example is the 1987 boycott of Burger King over its environmentally hazardous meat production, in which environmentalists sought to end Burger King's contracts with beef providers in the Central American Amazon rainforest.
[169] Simon Caney, 2015: 63, argues for an individual right to resist global injustice, including climate change, by a variety of means ranging from peaceful protests to harming property, even hacking into a company's or government's computer systems. While there is some overlap with soft war tactics, Caney's discussion of global justice is explicitly limited to individual modes of action that fall short of war and does not apply the just war framework as a whole.

Resorting to a mixture of *jus ad vim* and/or soft war tactics to combat environmental injustice is probably our best shot in terms of efficacy and proportionality, from both human- and non-human-centred ethical perspectives. From a traditional and legal standpoint, non-kinetic alternatives and soft power will be more appropriate against civilians and civilian infrastructure, however culpable they may be for the environmental wrongs in question.[170] Moreover, soft war tactics do not run the risk of counter-productiveness in terms of causing further environmental harm. Last resort and proportionality, as well as common sense, also require exhausting measures such as punitive economic sanctions of increasing severity and collective diplomatic pressures before contemplating force, particularly where no prior belligerent attack has taken place.[171]

When outright environmental aggression is perpetrated by an attacking army (as in the Russian case) or terrorist organizations (as in the case of Hamas), kinetic *jus ad vim* tactics against combatants and other military targets are legitimate, assuming reasonable chance of success, at a low cost to their operatives and to the natural surroundings they purport to protect. For revisionist philosophers of war, this conclusion holds also for targeting culpable civilian aggressors and applicable infrastructure, if attacking them is likely to reduce the injustice they cause while avoiding excessive costs to nature as well as to non-liable combatants and civilians on the just side.

2.3 Legitimate Authority and Right Intention

In conventional wars, the jus *ad bellum* condition of 'legitimate authority' appears virtually procedural, established automatically when war is declared by heads of state.[172] On whose authority would warfare or kinetic force short of war be waged on behalf of the environment, or humanity's interest in it? Few states are themselves environmentally compliant and therefore lack the moral standing to coerce (potentially by means of kinetic force) environmental bad actors, suggesting the appropriateness of forceful measures only in the most egregious cases.

Even *in extremis*, forceful measures to protect global resources or 'common heritage' should probably not be undertaken as lone ventures. Optimally, any military response to environmental wrongdoing would be an international endeavour rather than a vigilante job, subject to suspicions of ulterior motives. Possibly, as Craig Martin predicts in connection with climate change, combating environmental rogues would begin with demands on the UN Security

---

[170] Gross and Meisels, 2017: 33–48, esp. 41–48.
[171] Compare Martin, 2020: 376–77, on the precedent of economic sanctions against North Korea and Iran regarding nuclear proliferation.
[172] Lee, 2012: 82–83.

Council to authorize military action in advance under a widened understanding of its role in maintaining international peace and security before generating new 'just causes' for unilateral action, though how likely or desirable any of this is remains extremely questionable.[173] Martin argues persuasively that we ought to resist any such readjustments that would be counterproductive in terms of climate change and the international rule of law.[174] He also notes that 'The five permanent members of the U.N. Security Council are all among the most responsible for climate change'.[175]

Notwithstanding, counterproductivity may be mitigated by resorting to *jus ad vim* – drone strikes and targeted killing, cyber-attacks – which is less detrimental to the environment than large-scale warfare. Rule of law would still require, inter alia, satisfying the 'right authority' condition for any use of force. Acknowledging the dangers of opening a new cause for *jus ad bellum* (or *jus ad vim*), the UN Security Council, albeit nonideal, nonetheless seems the most 'legitimate authority' for protecting global resources – 'our common heritage' – from severe harm, when this is necessary at the bar of last resort.

Crucially, various soft war tactics can respond to 'environmental just cause' without opening the can of worms involved in authorizing military action on new pretexts. Affirming the protection of ecologically (as well as culturally) significant sites as 'a duty of justice', Fabre proposes a mixture of economic and international pressures, designed to combat defiant states.[176] While economic sanctions and expulsions from international organizations require authoritative decisions, they do not involve sanctioning war, lending these unarmed tactics an additional layer of justification that does not apply to *jus ad vim*. Moreover, some soft war pressure tactics are not subject to any formal political or legal constraints: individual boycotts, publicity and information warfare, nonviolent protest, and lawsuits may all be undertaken without appealing to any higher authority.

One further point regarding authorization is noteworthy. As with *jus ad vim*, soft war tactics have the additional advantage of carrying less risk for their agents, making them more likely candidates for approval by states and their international institutions. Militaries are naturally reluctant to risk their soldiers even to protect foreign civilians, let alone animals and ecosystems. *Jus ad vim* (targeted killing, drones, cyber-attacks) and soft war (conditional sales/purchases, boycotts, public protest, etc.) do not imperil soldiers and are relatively economical, freeing resources for other needs; they are therefore far more likely

---

[173] Martin, 2020: 374–78, 409.   [174] Martin, 2020: esp. 400–17.
[175] Martin, 2020: 409. On the US, see also Crawford, 2022.   [176] Fabre, 2021: 22.

to be authorized for environmental protection, at a lower moral cost to young lives and other assets.

Finally, beyond legitimate authority, warfare must also be undertaken with the right intentions, that is, those embedded in the war's just cause. Environmental war, not unlike humanitarian intervention, runs the risk of being used as a pretext for furthering other interests. International authorization mitigates this danger. Moreover, soft war and *jus ad vim* tactics that respect proportionality go a long way towards satisfying the rightful intention condition. In the event of an environmental wrong triggering the just cause requirement, it is incumbent on those combating it to demonstrate their sincerity by fighting in ways that avoid causing more environmental devastation than they prevent. Otherwise, they risk becoming aggressors themselves.[177]

2.4 Concluding Remarks

The laws of war focus on rules mitigating the conduct of hostilities rather than the reasons and nature of armed conflict, or justice of its cause. Consequently, within this sub-field – environmental ethics of war – pioneered primarily by lawyers, *jus ad bellum* has received even less consideration than the environmental ethics in war discussed in the previous section.

War's prima facie evil requires paying critical attention to any new justifications for armed conflict. Notwithstanding, ecological harm may sometimes constitute a just cause, at the intersection between human and non-human interests, even in the absence of bodily harm. The simplest cases of 'environmental aggression' that sit comfortably within the just war tradition are those in which borders are crossed, and environmental devastation involves territorial invasion and the destruction of property. At times, combatting environmental harms may accompany conventional defensive *casus belli*, enhancing the war's benefits and contributing to proportionality.

More controversially, in view of the ongoing environmental crisis, it is conceivable that a future just cause may arise from deliberate or negligent harm to the natural environment, even if no direct violence towards land or people has been perpetrated. This is where the fires in the Amazon rainforest came in. Examples like this also raise questions of legitimate authority, notably UN Security Council authorization.

Regarding proportionality *ad bellum*, where military response is apt and necessary, counter-measures must not wreak more environmental havoc than

---

[177] Compare Reichberg and Syse, 2000: 459. Without 'right intention': 'Victims of unjust aggression can swiftly become aggressors themselves.'

they purport to combat. I argued that both *jus ad vim* and soft war offer a better alternative for combating environmental wrongs than outright warfare. Both forceful measures short of war and soft war tactics are more likely to fulfil the requirement of *ad bellum* proportionality than large-scale armed conflict.[178]

Soft war begins with non-violent action – boycotts and 'media warfare', publicity and information, public pressure, as well as 'lawfare', i.e. international legal action against perpetrators of environmental harm.[179] Harsher unarmed measures include political–diplomatic pressure, possibly 'ecological peacekeeping', followed closely by economic restrictions and trade sanctions, such as 'green conditions' attached to loans, aid, and sales, and rising to cyber-warfare.[180] Most of these tactics may legitimately be employed against civilians as well as combatants, on all accounts of the just war tradition and international law. 'Just authority' is also irrelevant to most soft war tactics (with the likely exception of cyber-war), lending them an additional layer of justification.

Once non-kinetic measures have been exhausted, both environmental and humanitarian concerns about proportionality point towards resorting to limited force short of conventional war – *jus ad vim* – against military culprits and their infrastructure, preferably as a multinational task undertaken by an international authority.

Finally, satisfying proportionality in the case of an environmental just cause also goes towards fulfilling the further *jus ad bellum* criterion of 'right intention' by displaying sincere care for nature, rather than waging war for ulterior motives on an environmental pretext.

3 Environmental Ethics in Civil Wars

Most wars since 1945 have been intra-state conflicts, often occurring in areas containing the greatest biodiversity, and most wartime casualties since that time have occurred within them. The environment is no exception. By stark contrast, the prolific writing in JWT over the past few decades has concentrated almost exclusively on international conflicts, while notoriously neglecting the natural environment.[181] These two theoretical shortcomings coincide, as civil wars take

---

[178] Compare again: Betz, 2019: 238–41.   [179] Gross and Meisels, 2017: esp. 88–133, 152–83.
[180] Gross and Meisels, 2017: esp. 49–87. On 'ecological peacekeepers' and 'green conditionality', see Eckersley, 2007: 294, 302, 312.
[181] To take the classic case, Michael Walzer, 1977, makes little mention of civil war, apart from its references to the Lieber Code (1863). Recent exceptions to the neglect of civil war include Fabre, 2012: chap. 4; Lee, 2012: chap. 7; Parry, 2015.

place more often than their transnational counterparts on territories rich in natural resources.[182] 'Particularly troubling for conservationists is the fact that conflict zones very frequently coincide with so-called biodiversity hotspots',[183] Thor Hanson explains:

> For biodiversity conservation, the relevance of armed conflicts is confirmed by their prevalence in 'biodiversity hotspots,' regions that hold more than half the world's plant and animal species in only 2.3% of its land area. Between 1950 and 2000, over 90% of major armed conflicts took place within countries containing biodiversity hotspots, and more than 80% included fighting directly within hotspot areas.[184]

Moreover, human-induced environmental pressures and changes, often resulting in resource scarcity, may cause or enhance acute conflict, markedly in the developing world.[185] Anthropogenic climate change has been described as a 'threat multiplier' for political instability; the drought and subsequent migration preceding civil war in Syria is a controversial example.[186] Civil wars in Chad and Darfur are further cases in point.[187] Other scholars identify natural riches (especially oil), which are a source of funding and reward for rebels, as a partial cause of internal conflict.[188]

Combat itself adversely affects wildlife through the use of mines, bombs, and chemicals, often in already bio-sensitive habitats 'as were Rwanda's gorillas and Angola's elephants during and in the wake of these countries' respective civil wars'; 'mine triggers do not differentiate between humans and nontarget species of sufficient mass to activate them.'[189] The impact of the Rwandan civil war of 1994 on wildlife, accompanying the infamous human tragedy, is paradigmatic: bombs naturally killed all life forms indiscriminately, while mines reportedly placed along trails in Rwanda's Parc National des Volcans killed many gorillas.[190]

Years of civil war in Mozambique (1977–92) led to catastrophic die-offs of large mammal herbivores (elephants, zebras, buffalo, hippos, etc.), greatly

---

[182] Fabre, 2012: 135.   [183] Milburn and Van Goozen, 2021: 659.
[184] Hanson, 2018: 51; Hanson et al., 2009: 579–83; Milburn and Van Goozen, 2021.
[185] Homer-Dixon, 1991; Homer-Dixon, 1994.
[186] Bastien and Estève, 2018: 99; Duygu et al., 2018: 84–93; Gleick, 2014; Ide, 2018; Machlis and Hanson, 2008: 729; Selby et al., 2017.
[187] Alex and Estève, 2018.
[188] Bruch, 2001: 698; Collier and Hoeffler, 2004; Fearon and Laitin, 2003; Hourcle, 2001: 717–18, regarding Sierra Leone and Cambodia, funding belligerent activities, inter alia by extracting natural resources ('diamonds in Sierra Leone and timber in Cambodia', n. 136); Hanson et al., 2009: 584, on natural resources as a source of revenue for insurgents.
[189] Dudley et al., 2002: 323; Milburn and Van Goozen, 2021: 658; 2023: 424.
[190] Kanyamibwa, 1998: 1403–4.

decreasing their populations in African savannas, in turn affecting savanna habitats and resulting in biodiversity loss.[191] 'The elephants of Angola and Mozambique were widely hunted and killed during civil wars in those countries – the elephant population in Mozambique's Gorongosa National Park declined by 90% during the country's civil war.'[192] Trade in wildlife and animal products has served to fund many conflicts, particularly parties to civil wars.[193] Overall, 'A study of African protected areas found that the occurrence of armed conflict was the strongest predictor of a drop in large-mammal population sizes between 1946 and 2010'.[194]

As things stand, the most common and frequent environmental harms in sensitive regions – those caused by Non-International Armed Conflict (NIAC) specifically – receive only cursory ethical notice, or none at all, in the vast philosophical literature on the morality of war.[195] To date, no comprehensive ethics of war inquiry has been undertaken into the harsh effects of this predominant type of warfare on the natural environment.

Accordingly, this section focuses the 'environmental ethics of war' on civil conflict. Subsection 3.1 surveys the limited extent of international law of armed conflict applicable to civil strife, which is mostly lacking in its protection of the natural environment during NIAC. Subsection 3.2 elaborates on the overlap between conflict and biodiverse regions, as well as on the environmental hazards arising specifically from civil conflicts and in their aftermath. Subsection 3.3 sketches initial ethical guidelines for environmental protection in civil war and compares them with existing legal restrictions in international armed conflict.

Two caveats: first, for present purposes, 'civil war' refers loosely to all forms of domestic warfare – NIAC – occurring within a single state and among its members, with or without foreign intervention. In this sense, the common term 'civil war' is something of a misnomer, shorthand for the more encompassing but cumbersome technical term 'intrastate armed conflict'. Second, admittedly, beyond pure theory, any 'environmental philosophy of war', particularly for civil conflicts, is likely to inform international forces and institutions and influence guidelines for intervening armies, long before it applies directly to internal warring parties.

---

[191] Daskin et al., 2016: 79–80; and throughout ICRC, 2019. The 15-year civil war in Mozambique crushed the elephant population (among others) from 2000 to a mere 200.
[192] Milburn and Van Goozen, 2023: 424.   [193] Hanson, 2018: 54–55.
[194] Milburn and van Goozen, 2021: 659, citing Daskin and Pringle, 2018.
[195] The only exception I found within the scholarship of the morality of war is the brief but important mention of harm to animals in civil conflict by Milburn and Van Goozen, 2021: 658–59.

3.1 Environmental Law Applicable to NIAC

Only a small part of humanitarian law applies to NIAC. The laws that apply to NIAC – those laid down in Article 3 common to the Geneva Conventions (1949) and, more recently, Protocol II (1977) – aim to uphold civilian immunity and the rights of the sick and wounded, as well as to prohibit torture and further excesses in wartime.[196] They do not apply the full set of laws *in bello* applicable within international armed conflicts to non-international strife.

Lawyers note the limitations of the law applicable to NIAC, both with reference to overall deficiencies in Protocol II[197] and regarding environmental preservation specifically.[198] Designed for irregular forces or for regular forces fighting irregulars inside their own country, Protocol II sets up only minimal guarantees that do not include environmental provisions comparable to Additional Protocol I, while the 1977 Environmental Modification Techniques Convention (ENMOD) applies without prejudice to all types of conflict but is extremely narrow in scope, applying only to manipulation ('modification') of the environment.[199] The only indirectly relevant Protocol II provisions are Article 14 – protecting objects indispensable for the survival of the civilian population (agricultural areas, crops, livestock, drinking water installations, and irrigation works) – and possibly Article 15, which protects works and installations containing dangerous forces.[200]

Nonetheless, there is an emerging readiness on the part of major states and international forces to factor environmental concerns into the calculus of the military, and to apply the higher standards of international armed conflict, including their environmental aspects, to NIAC as well.[201] It is not always easy to clearly distinguish international from NIAC, particularly where

---

[196] Convention (III) Relative to the Treatment of Prisoners of War, Geneva, 12 August 1949: Conflicts Not of an International Character, Article 3; Protocol Additional to the Geneva Conventions of 12 August 1949 and Relating to the Protection of Victims of Non-International Armed Conflicts (Protocol II), 8 June 1977.

[197] Akande, 2012: 54; Bruch, 2001: 698; Cassese, 2008: 124; Cullen, 2010: 111; Green, 2018: 348–49; Hourcle, 2001: 680.

[198] Burger, 1996: 337–38; Bruch, 2001: 703, 709, 714–15; Hourcle, 2001: 680; Meron, 1996: ch. XX; Roberts, 2000: 76–77.

[199] Protocol I, Articles 35(3) and 55(1); Bruch, 2001: 703–4; Burger, 1996: 338; Richards and Schmitt, 1999: 1084; Schmitt, 1996: 262; 1997: 95.

[200] Burger, 1996: 338; Meron, 1996: 357, noting 'the anthropocentric provisions of Additional Protocol II (Articles 14–15) could be broadly interpreted to provide more direct protection to environmental assets'. Bruch, 2001: 714, even more remotely also notes that Article 16 protects cultural objects and places of worship; Article 17 prohibits the forced movement of civilians. Indirectly relevant provisions, notably Articles 14–17, might be invoked to prevent scorched earth, nuclear plants and chemical facilities, and protection of religiously significant areas.

[201] Burger, 1996, regarding the US, the UN, and NATO; Meron, 1996: 357–58. On environmental directives in military manuals, see also Schmitt, 1996: 243–44.

international and foreign forces are involved; this is an additional reason to apply the same legal regime to all cases.[202] Here, again, the general law of war principles and standards, necessity and proportionality, may have a further bearing on environmental protection in all types of armed conflict.[203] The continuing relevance of domestic environmental law is particularly pertinent in the case of internal strife, where the distinction between armed conflict and civil disturbances is less stark.[204]

Lawyers concerned with protecting the environment during NIAC concentrate on arguments and mechanisms for extending environmental protection in international wars (as well as peacetime regulation) to internal armed conflicts.[205] Advocating criminal liability for environmental damage in civil wars, Carl Bruch notes that 'While not directly applicable to internal conflicts, the norms applicable to international armed conflict constitute the most developed framework for constraining environmental damage from armed conflict'.[206] The virtually non-existent environmental regulation of NIAC prompts us to build on existing understandings, in ethics as well as law. The penultimate part of this section asks whether civil conflicts and insurgencies are morally subject to different environmental burdens or permissions at the bar of *jus in bello* from those that apply (or ought to apply) in traditional interstate wars.[207]

3.2 Civil Wars

To recap: civil wars are under-regulated – both generally and regarding the natural environment in particular – and their level of adherence to existing law is inferior. Armed conflict in the post-World War II era has been mostly intra-national, with over 80 per cent of such warfare between 1950 and 2000 occurring within biodiversity hotspots.[208] Both these features of contemporary conflict as well as their overlap have been largely overlooked by just war theorists, though less so in empirical studies. While hotspots represent less than 2 per cent of the earth's land, they support about half of the world's plants and many rare species.[209]

---

[202] Bruch, 2001: 707–8; Meron, 1996: 355.
[203] Bruch, 2001: 710; Meron, 1996: 353, 356; Roberts, 2000; Schmitt, 1997.
[204] Meron, 1996: 353.
[205] For example, in the above: Hourcle, 2001; Meron, 1996; Burger, 1996; Bruch, 2001, esp. Part II. As Meron, 353, notes: 'It is encouraging that there is an emerging consensus that acts prohibited in international wars should not be tolerated in civil wars.'
[206] Bruch, 2001: 701.
[207] Compare, *mutatis mutandis*, Fabre, 2012: chap. 4, 131, 135–41, esp. on 'special relationship' regarding *jus ad bellum* obligations; Parry, 2015.
[208] Kikuta, 2020: 1243; with reference to Hanson et al., 2009: 580. [209] ICRC, 2019.

Internal conflict and its aftermath are a major cause of deforestation, with considerable impact on biodiversity. Northern and Central Ethiopia, for example, have lost most of their tree cover through civil war.[210] Other prominent examples include the Great War of Africa in the Democratic Republic of the Congo (DRC), where over a five-year period civil war caused as much as a 1.61 per cent loss of forests (in both battle and non-battle zones), more than the entire territory of Belgium and nearly half that of Sierra Leone.[211]

Counter-insurgency, for its part, may require deforestation in conflict areas in order to eliminate insurgent hideouts (e.g. Turkish forces deliberately set fire to forests to reduce cover for Kurdish forces in their ongoing conflict with the PKK).[212] All warring parties have an incentive to mobilize resources such as timber, cutting down trees alongside exploitation of other natural supplies.[213] Abundant examples include 'rampant trade in "conflict" timber and diamonds during civil wars in Liberia, Sierra Leone, and elsewhere'.[214]

Displaced populations require resources for their survival during and after hostilities by 'living off the land' – poaching, foraging, looting, etc. – as do guerrilla forces.[215] In the DRC, conflict wiped out 95 per cent of hippos, as their habitats were destroyed and the animals could not be protected from poachers.[216] Nature reserves and national parks have been used for grazing, house-building, and hunting.[217] By the mid–late 1990s, 'An estimated 850,000 refugees from the Rwandan civil war were living in or around Virunga National Park' – Africa's most biodiverse protected area (in Zaire/DRC) – cutting down trees for wood, leading to massive environmental degradation, specifically deforestation.[218] After a decade of war and civil unrest, aerial surveys of the park 'found 629 hippopotami from a population that once exceeded 30,000 animals'.[219] Demand for firewood, charcoal, and building materials has led to similar land degradation and losses of forest and woodland around settlements of internally displaced Darfuris in Sudan, Somali refugees in Kenya, and Afghan refugees in Pakistan.[220]

War-related forest loss in Nicaragua, Columbia, as well as DRC and along the South Sudan–Uganda border, is attributed primarily to such changes in human

---

[210] Attfield, 2018: 75; on forest loss due to civil war in Cambodia, primarily in its aftermath, see: Ayram, 2021; Murillo-Sandoval et al., 2021; on deforestation in Rwanda, see Kanyamibwa, 1998: 1402–4.
[211] Kikuta, 2020: 1243, 1249, 1252–53; on Sierra Leone itself, see Lindsell et al., 2011: 69–77.
[212] Hanson, 2018: 53; Roberts, 2000: 75.   [213] Hanson, 2018: 54; Kikuta, 2020: 1250–52.
[214] Hanson, 2018: 53.   [215] Dudley et al., 2002: 322; Bruch, 2001: 698.   [216] ICRC, 2019.
[217] Kanyamibwa, 1998: 1403.
[218] Dudley et al., 2002: 325–26; Hanson, 2018: 55; Hanson et al., 2009: 584; Kanyamibwa, 1998: 1403.
[219] Machlis and Hanson, 2008: 731; Hanson et al., 2009: 584.   [220] Hanson, 2018: 55.

settlement and activity patterns.[221] In Rwanda, the south-eastern portion of the Nyungwe montane forest – dominated by bamboo and home to the owl-faced monkey – as well as other biodiverse mountain forests were largely cleared for agriculture.[222] While depopulation of conflict zones may have beneficial environmental effects, such as an increase in wildlife and reforestation, it is often counterbalanced by increased activity elsewhere, so that the overall consequences of armed conflict for biodiversity remain overwhelmingly negative.[223] Moreover, 'Some post war biodiversity impacts represent a straightforward continuation of effects begun during wartime, such as persistent deforestation near long-term refugee camps'.[224]

In all cases, the anthropogenic perspective, military necessity, and immediate human needs overshadow environmental considerations. Lack of environmental concern in the face of military imperatives and the importance of winning is particularly crucial in less-developed countries, particularly in Africa, where people are more dependent on natural resources,[225] and where losing may entail unforgiving repercussions. Developing nations are also more likely to experience internal conflict, as has been the case in Mozambique, Angola, Somalia, DRC, Sierra Leone, and Rwanda, conducted more frequently and less lawlessly than international wars, as well as more often within environmentally sensitive regions.[226]

In Rwanda specifically, as well as Darfur, Cambodia, and Sierra Leone, humanitarian tragedy not only takes priority over environmental issues but renders their mention slightly obscene. Notwithstanding, there is a growing realization that preserving the natural environment is also an urgent human interest, albeit in the longer term.[227] Moreover, as we have seen, often human and non-human concerns go hand in hand as the humanitarian crises accompanying and succeeding wars, including those involving refugees and displaced persons, can also have devastating impacts on wildlife and natural resources.[228]

Any practicable moral rules for protecting the natural environment in armed conflict – international and internal – require a delicate balance between multiple *in bello* and *post bellum* perspectives, recommending once again a moderate, conservative, all-encompassing approach. NIAC specifically raises unique challenges for balancing human and non-human interests and

---

[221] Hanson, 2018: 54.   [222] Kanyamibwa, 1998: 1403–4.
[223] Dudley et al., 2002: 319–22, 327 and *passim*; Hanson, 2018: 54, 58; Lindsell, 2011: 69–77. See also Milburn and Van Goozen, 2021: 658, on overall negative impact of warfare on wildlife.
[224] Hanson, 2018: 55.   [225] Kanyamibwa, 1998: 1399, 1405.
[226] Compare Kanyamibwa, 1998: 1399.   [227] Kanyamibwa, 1998: 58–59.
[228] Hanson et al., 2009: 584.

vulnerabilities, generating special responsibilities towards civilians and their natural surroundings.

3.3 Protecting the Natural Environment in Civil Conflict

Several distinct features of civil conflict suggest special moral obligations on the part of the warring parties towards the natural environment, as well as more general universal responsibilities on the part of combatants generally, including local and intervening forces.

First and foremost, as noted repeatedly, is their location: most civil wars take place within a tiny portion of the earth's land surface, typically rich in vertebrate life, containing rare species and (according to the Red Cross[229]) approximately 50 per cent of the world's plant life. In other words, they overlap to a very large extent with biodiversity hotspots. Moreover, civil wars often take place on territories rich in useful natural resources.

Moving on to participants, internal wars are fought between two or more parties within a state, all of whom bear special responsibilities towards that state's inhabitants, territory, and territorial resources. It is widely accepted that governments have protective duties towards their own population, whom they are sworn to protect. Writing of civil war, Vattel pointed out that

> we must, in the first place, recollect that all the sovereign's rights are derived from those of the state or of civil society, from the trust reposed in him, from the obligation he lies under of watching over the welfare of the nation, of procuring her greatest happiness, of maintaining order, justice, and peace within her boundaries.[230]

Rebels and freedom fighters also have special obligations towards members of the population they profess to be fighting for, as well as for their own homeland terrain, beyond general duties to refrain from harming civilians and their environment. Like governments, rebels derive any legitimacy they may have from the welfare of their people. Regardless of national partiality, rebels are responsible for their civilian co-nationals because they claim to act for them and in their name. This presumably includes due care for their natural surroundings and the resources necessary for their survival and well-being.

In reality, civilians caught up in local conflict are often abandoned by both rebels and sovereigns, remaining utterly defenceless, as well as emotionally forsaken by friends and relatives who find themselves in opposing camps. Whereas governments engaged in international wars aim to protect their civilian

---

[229] Hanson, 2018: 51; Hanson et al., 2009: 579–83; ICRC, 2019; Milburn and Van Goozen, 2021: 659.
[230] Vattel, 1758: Book III, chap. 18, para. 287.

population and distance the fighting from the home front, civil wars, by stark contrast, take place mostly among civilians within their environment, by parties concerned primarily with victory at all costs.

As for deleterious consequences, civil conflict typically lasts longer than interstate wars, with a higher level of devastation to civilians and their natural surroundings.[231] Fought typically to the bitter end rather than concluding in negotiated settlement,[232] local wars and their harmful effects are also likely to recur within the first decade after their conclusion.[233] Crucially, rebellions, revolutions, and insurgencies are fought mostly unconventionally,[234] adding costs to civilian environments, with guerrillas typically living amidst civilians and subsisting off the land.[235]

Civil wars, we have seen, are fought mostly outside any structure of rules, let alone any concern for the natural surroundings in which they are conducted. As noted, the extremely basic anthropocentric guidelines for protecting the environment set out in Protocol I do not apply to civil conflict, and even the humanitarian rudiments of Common Article 3 and Protocol II are largely ignored. Nonetheless, accounting for special relationships as well as location, a traditional military ethics perspective with an eye to the future suggests that civil wars ought to be subject to standards of environmental protection that are at least similar to, if not higher than, those of international armed conflict.

Conversely, Cecile Fabre argues that in the case of a just insurgency local civilians may be particularly liable to collateral harm because they are the potential beneficiaries of the war.[236] This would presumably include incidental damage to their natural environment. Moreover, rebels are typically disadvantaged in terms of weaponry and military resources, possibly justifying greater liberties on the part of the weaker side.[237]

At least from a revisionist perspective, when insurgents have a just cause they may conceivably be subject to a lower standard of *jus in bello* regulations, giving them a fighting chance against injustice.[238] Philosophically, revisionist theorists might argue that bona fide resistance movements can justify

---

[231] Collier and Hoeffler, 2004: 563–95; Collier et al., 2003: 11; Fabre, 2012: 135, 157; Kalyvas, 2006: 18, 54; Regan, 2002: 55–73.
[232] Collier et al., 2003: 11; Licklider, 1995: 681–87.
[233] Collier and Hoeffler, 2004: 563–95; Fearon and Laitin, 2003: 75–90; Henderson and Singer, 2000: 275–99; Kalyvas, 2006; Lacina, 2006: 276–89; Mason and Fett, 1996: 546–68; Walter, 1997: 335–64.
[234] Fearon, 2004: 298; Lee, 2012: 258–59. On lack of traditional battlefield: Kalyvas, 2006: 83; 2009: 427.
[235] Lee, 2012: 258–65.   [236] Fabre, 2012: 159–60.   [237] Compare Parry, 2015: sec. 3.
[238] Compare Gross, 2015, who suggests throughout that the laws of armed conflict ought to be adjusted more extensively and interpreted more liberally, to accommodate just insurgents, enabling them to fight legally against unjust regimes.

unavoidable harm to the environment by reference to the objective justness of their cause combined with the military asymmetry of the conflict and the potential benefit of victory to local inhabitants. Fending off genocide, to take the extreme example, would clearly generate such extra licence on all existing accounts of (anthropocentric) JWT.[239] Any other conclusion, favouring nature over human life, would far exceed overlapping consensus as advocated in Section 1.

In many other cases, however, difficulties in establishing objective and absolute justice on one side or another, particularly in complex multi-party internal conflicts, as well as the prospect of enforcing it on the warring factions, may preclude the possibility of deriving any useful rules of conduct from such deep moral insight.

Intrastate wars being what and where they are, any environmental requirements will, at most, set standards and command respect from international organizations and intervening forces and guide oversight and post-war accountability, rather than effectively enforcing first-order rules on the warring parties themselves, whether just or unjust. This is, nonetheless, no small achievement. Advocating the conduct towards the environment displayed by intervening forces in former Yugoslavia as a future model, US Colonel James Burger argues for equal application of environmental rules to all situations.[240] The presence of international peacekeeping forces challenges the distinction between intranational and international conflict, as well as between wartime and peacetime environmental rules. Moreover, intervening forces are out there to protect, and therefore bear a particularly heavy burden of obligation to refrain from making matters worse. At the same time, they often face considerable challenges, which brought on their intervention to begin with, in protecting human life, even at a cost to the environment.

Overall, the variety of exceptional circumstances listed above imply that combatants engaged in civil conflict – both local and foreign – albeit facing unique hardships, nonetheless shoulder a particularly high level of environmental responsibility. This holds not only for non-anthropocentric environmental ethics that attach intrinsic value to the environment (its life forms or ecology) but *also* from a human-centred perspective, attributing instrumental value to the environment in terms of utility. The law of war protects the natural environment not only because of its intrinsic value but because it sustains human life.[241]

Locals, both governments and rebels, have fiduciary duties of care towards the population whom they purport to represent and propose to govern, which

---

[239] We believe this is a safe assumption, even without invoking Walzer, 1977: chap. 16: 'Supreme Emergency'.
[240] Burger, 1996.   [241] ICRC, 2019.

must include their natural surroundings and resources – present and future – and natural objects for their survival and well-being. From a non-cosmopolitan perspective, both insurgents and soldiers also have special obligations stemming from national affiliation and partiality towards fellow citizens and their homeland terrain.

Universal obligations command everyone to pay special attention to biodiversity conservation in armed conflict, particularly in biologically rich regions. Intervening parties are better informed and equipped to recognize and follow environmental rules.[242] Their very presence calls into question the distinction between NIAC and international wars, suggesting the applicability of Protocol I standards. Peacekeeping forces, as well as the necessarily continuous demands of care for the natural environment, blur the distinction between wartime and peacetime rules. Revisionist philosophers of war reject such distinctions in any event.[243]

3.4 Concluding Remarks

Just war theory and the morality of war have been applied far less to internal armed conflict than to conventional wars between states, as well as devoting very little attention to the environmental aspect of armed conflict. The two deficiencies overlap. Non-international armed conflict has long become the norm for warfare rather than the exception, with considerable consequences for the natural environment, for example in Angola, Cambodia, and Colombia.[244] These concerns are brought together in the geographical overlap between internal armed conflict and areas with high biological richness and limited extent.[245] At the same time, existing international law provides only a few environmental protections during internal armed conflicts.[246]

The more developed law of international armed conflict is morally instructive but not definitive. Civil wars are different in several respects from international conflicts, and these differences may have a moral bearing on their regulation. Considering the demands of justice regarding the environment specifically in intrastate as opposed to interstate wars suggests an equal, if not higher, responsibility to protect in the case of NIAC.

---

[242] Compare Burger, 1996. [243] See e.g. McMahan, 2012; Parry, 2015: sec. 2.1.
[244] Bruch, 2001: 706, 720.
[245] Definition in Hanson et al., 2009: 579. See also 583: 'Our analysis revealed a startling pattern. Armed conflicts were highly prevalent and consistent in the world's most biologically important regions, underscoring the urgency of understanding the effects of warfare in the context of biodiversity conservation.'
[246] Bruch, 2001: 699.

On a practical note, given the nature of civil conflicts and their participants, it is hard enough to impose minimal humanitarian standards, let alone enforce environmental regulations. Any emerging guidelines and rules of engagement in this field are more likely to inform intervening forces and instruct international institutions – both common to NIAC – than to apply directly as first-order rules to warring factions, at least for the foreseeable future.[247]

4 Environmental Terrorism

Environmental disruption and degradation are old features of war, but the term 'environmental terrorism' is relatively new, dating back to the Persian Gulf War oil spills and subsequent fires in Kuwaiti oil fields.[248] Academic interest in terrorism surfaced mostly after 9/11, with notable late twentieth-century exceptions.[249] The increase in environmental awareness is more recent still.

This section examines the relatively novel and ambiguous term 'environmental terrorism', combining insights from both terrorism scholarship and environmental politics, ultimately drawing lessons for the here and now. Subsection 4.1 considers the definitions of terrorism more generally and argues that a useful characterization will indicate why terrorism is wrong. Following Michael Walzer, I suggest that terrorism is the intentional murder of random civilians for political purposes.[250] Subsection 4.2 considers various distinct meanings of 'environmental terrorism' in particular. Subsequently, Subsection 4.3 asks whether the natural world can fully qualify as a victim of terrorism. In keeping with the rejection of 'environmental non-combatant immunity' in Subsection 1.3, this subsection argues that, absent human targets, deliberately destroying nature does not in itself meet the requirements of 'terrorism'. Finally, Subsection 4.4 asks what would constitute an appropriate and proportionate response to 'environmental terrorism'.

One timely example comes from the Gaza Strip. On 30 March 2018, protesters in Gaza instigated a civil resistance campaign along the border with Israel. Following these border disturbances, Gazans launched countless kites, and (as of May 2018) party balloons and inflated latex condoms bearing flammable materials and explosives – grenades, Molotov cocktails, etc. – into Israeli territory. Though these attacks never resulted in Israeli fatalities, they

---

[247] Machlis and Hanson, 2008: 733–34: 'policy outcomes are most relevant to traditional states with organized armed forces; they are less relevant to nonstate guerrilla groups, rogue states, and terrorist organizations.'

[248] Chalecki, 2002: 46; 2020: 63; Seacor, 1994: 522, n. 218, referring to Lee, 1991: 386; Schwartz, 1998: 483, 492.

[249] Exceptions include Laqueur, 1987; Netanyahu, 1986; 2001; Schmid, 1984; Schmid and Jongman, 1988; esp. Walzer, 1977: 176–206; Wilkins, 1992.

[250] Walzer, 1977: 197, 203; 2006.

sparked fires burning thousands of acres of farmland, parks, forests, and nature reserves, killing animals, destroying beehives, wildlife and natural habitats, and wreaking ecological devastation in the Western Negev with long-term environmental ramifications.[251] On one occasion, a burning falcon outfitted with a harness carrying flaming material was propelled from Gaza into Israel.[252] In June 2018, kites from Gaza destroyed vast parts of the Carmia nature reserve inside Israel, causing massive damage.[253]

Continuing seasonally into 2021, and recurring in Fall 2023 (a mere two weeks before the October 7 massacre), airborne arson attacks caused economic and psychological harm, spread fear, and disrupted daily life.[254] Many of the incendiary devices found inside Israel were coloured as party balloons with cartoon decorations, apparently aimed at attracting children;[255] some fell in residential areas and within family homes.[256] Israel dubbed these attacks 'balloon terrorism', 'terror kites' and 'arson terror', exploring the legality and expediency of various counter-terrorism measures in response.[257]

Terrorism is a contested concept, associated primarily with the murder and maiming of civilians; its applicability to environmental destruction is far from obvious. The following subsection argues that the term 'terrorism' is partly rhetorical in environmental contexts. Acts of hostility directed exclusively at non-human elements of the natural world may not in and of themselves constitute terrorism. In principle, this section suggests, the moral condemnation of terrorism ought rightly to be reserved for the indiscriminate targeting of human non-combatants. At the same time, the severity of environmental harm should not be understated. Attacking the natural environment during armed conflict is arguably a war crime. Moreover, in reality, hostile acts against nature may go so far towards threatening civilians as to constitute bona fide terrorism, as well as going hand in glove with attacking non-combatants more directly.

4.1 What Is Terrorism and What Is Wrong with It?

Terrorism has countless definitions, each with its own objective and agenda. There are by now equally numerous remarks to this effect, especially since 9/11. There is to date no canonical, universally agreed definition of terrorism, whether legally, philosophically, or in ordinary usage. It has become almost

---

[251] Zych, 2019: 76; Stefanini, 2021: 664, 674. [252] Moodrick-Even Khen, 2019: 329.
[253] *Times of Israel*, 2018; Zych, 2019: 78.
[254] Dahman et al., 2023; Moodrick-Even Khen, 2019: 332; Stefanini, 2021: 674; Yadlin, 2018: 2; Zych, 2019: 78–79.
[255] Zych, 2019: 75. [256] Moodrick-Even Khen, 2019: 329; Stefanini, 2021: 670.
[257] Moodrick-Even Khen, 2019: 331–34; Stefanini, 2021: 669, 673; Yadlin, 2018: 2–3; Zych, 2019: 79–81.

commonplace to suggest that definition is impossible and redundant – 'we know it when we see it' – or sectarian – 'one man's terrorist is another's freedom fighter' – or meaningful only within specific fields (law, finance, sociology) for specific purposes.[258] Others propose 'neutral objective' all-encompassing definitions that include various forms of political violence and a mixture of historical cases, concluding effectively that terrorism is in the eye of the beholder.[259]

Various features are typically listed in association with terrorism, notably its theatrical–media element and audience,[260] illegality, targeting civilians, 'weapon of the weak',[261] political goals, causing fear and panic. But terrorism scholars differ, and often remain undecided, regarding any necessary and sufficient conditions. The broadest 'non-biased' definitions of terrorism include various forms of illegal political violence that fall short of war,[262] the terrorizing acts of states in war, as well as 'state terrorism' towards the states' own citizenry[263] or enemy civilians. Others add institutional 'structural violence', often associated with capitalism and globalization.[264]

These inclusive definitions do not necessarily condemn 'terrorism' as such, encompassing a wide mixture of historical cases – ranging from American and French revolutionaries to the Maquis, Irgun and Stern Gang, the atomic bombs on Japan, structural inequality, Bush and Blair, Hamas, and ISIS. Such theorists take pride in objectivity, criticizing stricter definitions for building 'a judgment of immorality, or non-justifiability into the definition of terrorism, making it impossible even to question whether given acts of terrorism might be justified'.[265]

Evaluating the changing character of war and terrorism, as well as appropriate counter-measures, requires clearer insight. It is, Aristotle teaches, our capacity to distinguish and define which enables us to make ethical judgments.[266] As Tony Coady puts it: 'There are two central philosophical questions about terrorism: What is it? And what, if anything, is wrong with it? Here I propose to deal with the first question, but I do so because of the importance of the second.'[267]

Terrorism is a pejorative term. In keeping with common usage, a good definition will indicate what is wrong with terrorism, and strictly specify which new incidents fall within this derogatory category and which do not.

---

[258] Chalecki, 2002: 47; Fletcher, 2006; Waldron, 2004: 6.
[259] For example Chomsky, 2001; Derrida in Borradori, 2003; Goodin, 2006; Held, 2004; Honderich, 1989; 2002; Young, 2004.
[260] Chalecki, 2002: 47; Fletcher, 2006: 16.   [261] For example, Young, 2004.
[262] Honderich, 2002: 98–99.   [263] Goodin, 2006: esp. 179–80.
[264] Derrida in Borradori, 2003: 107–8.   [265] Held, 2004: 65.
[266] Aristotle, 1976: 75–76, Books I–VII.   [267] Coady, 2004: 3.

'Environmental terrorism' is a paradigm case in point. While the broadest definitions may charitably include harm to the environment under the rubric of terrorism, they will not necessarily attach any negative judgement to this label and cannot teach us much about its normative implications.

Michael Walzer's critical understanding of terrorism in his seminal *Just and Unjust Wars* provides the classic definition, which has become the term of reference for practically every discussion on terrorism. According to Walzer, 'terrorism' is the random killing of innocent people, generating pervasive fear for a variety of political purposes.[268] Killing non-combatants at random is a crucial element, referring both to the violation of civilian immunity and to the total disregard for the identity of the victim.[269] Randomness sets terrorism apart from milder forms of political violence – guerrilla warfare directed at armies and political assassination aimed at state officials.[270] Attacking anyone within a political community, rather than selected individuals, Walzer explains, not only increases fear but also delivers a devaluating, uncompromising message of rejection to an entire group: *'We don't want you here'*.[271] Hamas's indiscriminate onslaught on October 7, conveying the message 'from the river to the sea', is a gruesomely clear example.

Walzer's censorious depiction of terrorism as the terrifying random murder of innocent civilians for political gain is echoed in countless modern works.[272] Most authors also include fear – literal terrorization – in their definitions of terrorism. Tied at the philological level to the term itself, this basic feature – intended and resulting fear – cuts across political lines and is included in the widest variety of discussions on terrorism.[273] Moreover, Jurgan Habermas noted after 9/11, terrorism (as opposed to paramilitary guerrilla tactics) 'revolves around murder, around the indiscriminate annihilation of enemies, women and children – life against life', and can never be legitimized.[274]

No doubt, Walzer acknowledges, 'the use of the term is contested; that's true of many political terms. The use of "democracy" is contested, but we still have, I think, a pretty good idea of what democracy is. ... The case is the same with terrorism.'[275] Terrorism is essentially about targeting random non-combatants, along with anyone else, instilling pervasive fear in civilians as a means to

---

[268] Walzer, 1977: 197, 203; 2006.
[269] Coady, 2004: 7; Primoratz, 2004: 18; Walzer, 2006b: 3.   [270] Walzer, 1977.
[271] Walzer, 2006b: 5.
[272] To name just a few: Berman, 2003: 35–36; Borradori, 2003: 35, 56; Coady, 2001: 1697; 2004: 3–14; Gilbert, 2003: 96–97; Leiser, 1986: 155; 2004; Meisels, 2006: 472–78; 2008: 20–29; 2009: 341–48; Netanyahu, 1986: 9, 132; 2001, xxi, 8; Primoratz, 2004: xii, 15–30; Smilansky, 2004: 790.
[273] Netanyahu, 1986: 9, 132; 2001: 8; Walzer, 1977: 197, 203; 2006.
[274] Habermas in Borradori, 2003: 33, 56.   [275] Walzer, 2002; Walzer, 2004: 131.

political ends. This basic understanding allows for variation and has some fuzzy edges, but it is, at the very least, its core content.

It remains to be seen whether environmental destruction can qualify as terrorism in this sense: under what conditions, and to what degree, it shares the normative shortcomings of terror, as well as how to respond. I begin with what is wrong with terrorism in the narrow sense defined in this subsection.

Terrorism, Walzer and Habermas maintain, devalues entire nations or classes, and attacks the defenceless among them, violating the most basic rule of the just war tradition.[276] Beyond conventions of war, terrorism defies a key standard of liberal humanist morality, at least from Kant through Rawls, which fundamentally forbids the use of human beings as means only, and prescribes their treatment as ends in themselves.[277] It also violates an older cross-cultural commitment to protect the defenceless and vulnerable, those who are not trained to fight or cannot fight, namely women, children, clergymen, and elderly people, who are disengaged from military activity.[278]

Terrorism is also a form of free riding. 'Terrorism of the weak' relies on conventional armies observing traditional rules of war, while the terrorists themselves thwart them. If their stronger adversaries were to match the terrorists' nihilism by denying civilian immunity, choosing to terrorize the latter with their superior force, they would once again have the upper hand, rendering ineffective the smaller-scale terrorism of the 'underdog'. Terrorism wholly depends upon its opponents upholding a moral code that the terrorists themselves reject. Terrorists also rely on a set of civil liberties, which they often hold in contempt, but which enables them to operate more freely than they could in their absence. Terrorism's very effectiveness depends on a reversal of the Kantian imperative to 'act only on that maxim through which you can at the same time will that it should become a universal law'.[279]

Regardless of its professed cause, terrorism in the strict sense – murdering random civilians as a political strategy – is diametrically opposed to the requirements of liberal morality and is defensible only at the cost of relinquishing the most basic of liberal commitments. None of this condemnation applies to attacks on natural resources and environmental destruction for political gain.

4.2 Environmental Terrorism: Assorted Meanings

The most obvious difference between traditional terrorism and 'environmental terrorism' specifically is that the former is aimed directly at human beings,

---

[276] Habermas in Borradori, 2003: 33, 56; Walzer, 1977: 203; 2006: 5.
[277] Kant, 1964: 96; Rawls, 1989: 179.   [278] Berman, 2003: 98; Walzer, 1977: 43.
[279] Kant, 1964: 88.

whereas the latter targets other inhabitants of the natural world, addressing and affecting humans only indirectly and with varying degrees of severity. Typical examples include the destruction of forests and agricultural sites by fire. 'Dry weather conditions can make forests, fields, and grasslands more susceptible to fire' and hence make them a prime target with potentially devastating economic and environmental consequences.[280] The fires sparked by Hamas's arson attacks in the Israeli South between 2018 and 2023 are cases in point. Attacks aimed specifically at the agricultural sector are often classified as 'agro-terrorism', alongside the use of biological agents against domestic animals and crops.[281]

In contrast to the post-9/11 surge in terrorism scholarship, the relevant literature on its environmental brand is relatively scant and scattered across various academic fields, from law to political science, geopolitics, and environmental ethics. Several clarifications are in order, regardless of discipline.

First, environmental terrorism is distinct from 'eco-terrorism' – violence carried out to further ecological causes – though the labels are occasionally used interchangeably.[282] For eco-terrorists advancing an environmentalist agenda, the environment is an objective (e.g. saving the planet) rather than a target.[283] Examples include militant environmental groups such as the Earth Liberation Front (ELF) and its sister organization the Animal Liberation Front (ALF), believed to be responsible for some 600 criminal acts between 1996 and 2002.[284] Illegal violence notwithstanding, much 'eco-terrorism' does not maim or kill, often aiming instead at property considered ecologically detrimental; its classification as 'terrorism' rather than sabotage (or 'ecotage') is therefore debatable.[285]

As opposed to 'eco-terrorism', 'environmental terrorism' more often refers to the deliberate destruction or manipulation of the natural environment in the name of political or ideological zealotry.[286] Like environmental warfare, environmental terrorism involves attacking or utilizing the forces of nature for hostile purposes.[287] This includes targeting natural resources directly, such as by incendiary means, as well as harnessing elements of the environment itself as *tools* of war or terror.[288] An example of the latter is the means and methods of warfare prohibited by the 1977 Environmental Modification Techniques Convention (ENMOD), which bars using the environment itself (changing or

---

[280] Chalecki, 2002: 56; cf. Zych, 2019: 78; Stefanini, 2021: 670. [281] Zuber, 2015.
[282] For example, Edgerton, 1992. [283] Chalecki, 2002: 48–49; O'Lear, 2003: 139–43.
[284] Chalecki, 2002: 48–49; Leader and Probst, 2003: 37–38; Spadaro, 2020: 58.
[285] Loadenthal, 2017: 1–34; Spadaro, 2020: 57–58.
[286] Schofield, 1999: 619; Spadaro, 2020: 59.
[287] Schofield, 1999: 619–20; Westing, 1985: 646.
[288] O'Lear, 2003: 138; Schofield, 1999: 619.

manipulating natural processes, such as the weather) as a weapon. Biological and chemical warfare is another example of harnessing elements of the environment for hostile purposes.[289]

Similarly, the environment can be, and has been, harnessed as a conduit of attack – a delivery vehicle carrying destruction to a human population – such as the poisoning of water supplies.[290] Other times, 'the environment or resources themselves are targeted for destruction or compromise, with the collateral damage being felt by the population the terrorists wish to impact'.[291] In the former we might say the environment is a casualty, whereas in the latter the casualty is the directly targeted victim.[292]

Offering an eight-pronged taxonomy of environmental destruction, Daniel Schwartz suggests we reserve the term 'environmental terrorism' only for those acts of violence in which the *deliberate* manipulation of the environment is intended to instil trepidation in the larger population, specifically from the ecological consequences of the act.[293] This excludes unintended environmental damage and wanton vandalism, but also the most deliberate harnessing of natural resources for terroristic purposes. On this account, terroristic manipulation of nuclear, biological, or chemical materials (e.g. the use of nerve gas in the Tokyo subway) would not count as environmental terrorism because the perpetrators do not primarily intend to instil fear of the specifically ecological consequences of their act. In these cases, Schwartz argues, the environment is merely a casualty rather than a victim. The same goes for the purposeful wartime destruction of resources, such as scorched-earth policies, and even 'ecocide' – substantially damaging/destroying ecosystems – where the environmental destruction is strategic rather than symbolic, as the perpetrator is not attempting to create fear of the environmental consequences of the act, but is rather using the environment strategically to further other political ends.[294] On this account, Saddam Hussein's ecological destruction during the Persian Gulf War would not, contra President Bush's labelling, count as state terrorism because 'the Iraqi leader never issued an ecological threat and never "held the environment hostage"'.[295]

Quite narrowly construed, Schwartz's single example of 'environmental terrorism' is a 1995 incident in which a group of disgruntled fishermen on the Galapagos Islands – unhappy about an imposed limit on the lucrative trade of

---

[289] O'Lear, 2003: 138; Schofield, 1999: 628–33.
[290] Chalecki, 2002: 52; Schofield, 1999: 633–35.　[291] Chalecki, 2002: 52.
[292] Chalecki, 2002: 57; O'Lear, 2003: 140–43.　[293] Schwartz, 1998: 488.
[294] Schwartz, 1998: 491–92.
[295] Schwartz, 1998: 491. Others dispute the terrorism label in this case on the grounds that disrupting the environment to use it as tool of war is more akin to environmental warfare than to terrorism (Spadaro, 2020: 63).

sea cucumber harvesting – threatened, tortured, and killed 81 of the islands' rare tortoises.[296] Only this type of unlawfulness, Schwartz concludes, in war/peacetime, constitutes environmental terrorism *stricto sensu* 'because it is only in these scenarios that a perpetrator attempts to instil fear in the larger population over the ecological consequences of their destruction. In such cases the environment is the primary symbol, and ecology is a *victim* rather than a *casualty*.'[297]

More commonly, the label 'environmental terrorism' refers to all military or paramilitary violence that intentionally utilizes or targets natural resources to attain any political ends. This includes deliberate environmental destruction employed as a tactic to pressure governments or their citizenry to make political concessions, to seek retaliation for propaganda purposes, to attract attention to a political cause, or to convey a 'theatrical' message to one's enemy, fellow nationals, or the world at large. In environmental attacks, elements of the non-human world – be they forests, fields, rivers, or whatever form they take – are the direct victims of hostilities, though the ultimate political target remains humans. Whether such acts destroy resources or use them as a channel of attack, they may serve to symbolize the perpetrator's grievance, to instil fear in a civilian population, to intimidate the enemy into capitulation, to raise awareness to the assailants' political agenda, or to enlist supporters and activists to their cause. Groups such as ISIS in Syria and Iraq, for example, have 'shown their capacity to leverage the environment, by targeting water resources as tools to manipulate the population'.[298]

Several scholars suggest that existing legal doctrines 'fail to adequately respond to the specific threat of environmental terrorism'.[299] In the context of armed conflict, existing Geneva conventions prohibit intentionally targeting natural resources unless there is a direct military advantage to doing so.[300] As

---

[296] Schwartz, 1998: 489–90.
[297] Schwartz, 1998: 494. Read in context, the paper's central political contention is that the US Bush administration abused the concept for rhetorical purposes when it accused Saddam Hussein of 'environmental terrorism' (Schwartz, 1998: 493).
[298] Spadaro, 2020: 59.   [299] Schofield, 1999: 642; Seacor, 1994.
[300] Chalecki, 2002: 50; Reichberg and Syse, 2000: 450; Schmitt, 1996: 245–50; Seacor, 1994: 513–15; cf. Woods, 2007: 18. This is arguably less true of Protocol I (and ENMOD) provisions, 'in that no military necessity or proportionality balancing is required prior to its prohibitions taking effect' (Richards and Schmitt, 1999: 1062–63; Schmitt, 1996: 259–62). At the same time, 'the environmental provisions of the former [Protocol I] are not binding on the world's major military power and the scope of the latter is extraordinarily narrow. Second ... lack of environmental specificity forces us to fall back upon traditional law of war principles such as necessity and proportionality' (Richards and Schmitt, 1999: 1084; Schmitt, 1996: 262; 1997: 95; cf. Reichberg and Syse, 2000: 450). On balancing environmental damage with military necessity, see Jensen, 2005: 147, 177–79, and Schwabach, 2000: 139. Schmitt, 1997: 76, notes US refusal to ratify Protocol I, emphasizing specific objection to those provisions directed at environmental protection. Moreover, unlike some other Protocol I provisions, 'it is premature to assert that customary law in the classic sense has surfaced' (Schmitt, 1997: 76), remaining

noted in Section 1, this is clearly far weaker than the absolute prohibition of intentionally attacking civilians, which holds regardless of military advantage.[301] Nevertheless, terrorism is by definition indiscriminate violence, and 'because it is directed at a symbolic target, does not create an immediate military advantage for the attacker'.[302] Absent a direct military advantage, does targeting natural resources for indirect or symbolic purposes – such as to intimidate, coerce, or convey a political message – constitute terrorism?

Sometimes this question lacks practical significance, as when hostilities target civilians and their environment or destroy valuable or scarce resources, or when environmental damage severely prejudices civilian well-being and livelihood in violation of Additional Protocol I, Article 55.[303] These cases violate human civilian immunities rather than purely environmental interests. Consider resource destruction that also leads quite directly to loss of human life,[304] deliberately targets civilians within their environment, or causes arguably disproportionate long-term harm. In Kuwait, for example, 'The oil fires also signified a more menacing threat: their lasting impact on the environment and population of the region'.[305]

In the case of Gaza, Israel's resort to terrorism discourse to describe the fires emanating from the Strip is largely justified. Though there were no human casualties in the incendiary attacks, the aerial explosives from Gaza were equally designed to target random civilians, and some did in fact land in educational institutions, including the yard of a preschool facility, and in private houses causing property damage.[306] Dressing airborne explosive devices as children's toys indicates a clear intent to injure. Gazan activists evidently had no qualms about harming both natural resources and non-combatants within a single operation. When they ignited a field, if a couple of children had turned up to collect a colourful inflammatory kite or pick up an explosive party balloon, terrorists would not view this as a fly in the ointment or unfortunate collateral damage, but rather as a well sought-after added bonus.[307] Terrorism is indiscriminate in this sense as well: it is indifferent to the nature of its victim.

In principle, however, does targeting natural resources exclusively – to convey a message of fear, gain attention or political objectives, oppose oppression, or rally support – tick all the boxes of 'terrorism'? As noted in Section 1, the natural environment shares several features frequently associated with the

---

arguable (Gardam, 2004: 133). See also Richards and Schmitt, 1999: 1055, 1063 n. 65 and Hourcle, 2001: 672, 687.
[301] Reichberg and Syse, 2000: 450; Schmitt, 1996: 245–50.   [302] Schwartz, 1998: 486–87.
[303] Compare Chalecki, 2002: 52–55.   [304] Schwartz, 1998: 494.   [305] Seacor, 1994: 482.
[306] Compare Stefanini, 2021: 664, 670; Moodrick-Even Khen, 2019: 329.
[307] Compare Primoratz, 2004: 20.

victims of terror, among them the vulnerability of non-combatants and a lack of direct involvement in combat – connecting immunity from attack with military disengagement.

Nature is usually a non-military target, and attacking it often involves the destruction of civilian assets – both private and public. With growing environmental awareness, such attacks have increasing potential to cause fear and panic and attract public media attention to a particular cause.[308] In terms of 'violence as communication'[309] – theatre and conveying a message for political gain – as well as illegality, attacking the natural environment scores highly in its resemblance to hard-core terrorism.[310] As for potential harm, Timothy Schofield notes that 'Killing the horticulture of an ecosystem [notably by incendiary means] ... can cause substantial damage to that system's wildlife and topsoil. Recovery from such ecological damage could take decades.'[311] In terms of range and 'ongoing-ness', environmental damage scores higher than most terrorist attacks.

The question remains: 'If a bomb goes off in a forest and there is no one there to lose a view or to suffer collateral damage, is it terrorism? This raises questions of how and by whom the environment is valued, and on what time scale these values are identified.'[312]

4.3 Targeting Nature

Ethical evaluation of 'environmental terrorism' invariably intertwines not only with the controversial terrorism scholarship discussed above, but also with the variety in ethics of the environment, as discussed in Section 1. Absent human targets, does an assault on the natural world carry the negative normative baggage associated with 'terrorism'? This depends not only on our definition of terrorism but again on our classification of the non-human victim as compared with the human non-combatants most often identified as the targets of terror.

Critiquing 'environmental terrorism', Shannon O'Lear notes, regarding legal definitions, that targets of terrorism typically consist of non-combatants.[313] 'Considering the role the environment might have in this definition of terrorism, environmental areas or resources such as forests, water supplies, national parks, etc. would fall under the category of "noncombatant targets" and could be involved in terrorist activity in ways that would "influence an audience".'[314]

---

[308] See Chalecki, 2002: 51–52 on terrorism and media; O'Lear, 2003: 136 regarding conveying a message.
[309] Compare Schmid and de Graaf, 1982.   [310] Compare O'Lear, 2003: 133, 136.
[311] Schofield, 1999: 635–36; cf. Chalecki, 2002: 59.   [312] O'Lear, 2003: 138
[313] O'Lear, 2003: 133.   [314] O'Lear, 2003: 133.

Similarly, Elizabeth Chalecki argues ostensibly that 'Terrorism clearly violates the *jus in bello* criterion, since targeting non-combatants lies at the very core of its strategy. That the target is environmental and not human does not blur the distinction between warfare and terrorism.'[315] At the same time, she notes that prohibitions on intentionally attacking the environment are subject to military necessity.[316] This is patently not the case with *jus in bello* concerning human civilian immunity, which applies absolutely.

On Chalecki's account, deliberately burning forests or fields, setting a nature reserve ablaze, killing animals, destroying natural habitats, and so forth for political purposes, all target 'non-combatants', violating their immunity, and would *ipso facto* probably constitute acts of terrorism.

Can the environment count as a non-combatant, warranting its absolute protection on a par with civilian immunity, and labelling its violation as 'terrorism'? Adopted categorically, environmental non-combatant immunity would preclude not only wanton destruction but also absolutely any direct attacks on, or use of, the environment in wartime. Section 1 argued against extending non-combatant status to the environment as untenable for the law of armed conflict, while emphasizing its prima facie protection from direct attack, subject to military necessity, and the strong significance of environmental damage in determining proportionality.[317] This, however, remains a far cry from automatically branding purely environmental destruction as a violation of non-combatant immunity or genuine acts of terror.

One danger of the 'environmental terrorism' label is the risk of over-zealous environmentalism belittling the value of human life. Regarding acts that target humans within their environment or affect them profoundly, Schwartz warns that 'To label this act "environmental terrorism" might serve to elevate ecological concerns over concerns of human life. Although the ecological destruction might ultimately threaten human life, there is a danger in elevating the importance of this eventuality over the immediate loss of human life.'[318] Similarly, classifying purely environmental attacks as 'terrorism' runs the same risk of depreciating the value of human individuals, equating them with natural resources. One does not need to be an overly human-centred moral philosopher to note the difference between on the one hand killing or kidnapping children, or dismembering and butchering civilians, and on the other hand attacking a tree or a fossil formation, destroying a beehive, or arguably even abusing and killing a falcon or 81 rare tortoises.

---

[315] Chalecki, 2002: 49.   [316] Chalecki, 2002: 49.   [317] Hedahl et al., 2017: 437.
[318] Schwartz, 1998: 494.

From a liberal perspective, nothing like a Walzerian absolute anti-terrorism stance is applicable to flora and fauna, or even animals. For Kant (and Rawls) certainly, the categorical prohibition on using human beings as means only, prescribing their treatment as ends in themselves, does not extend to non-human inhabitants of the natural world.[319] Only human individuals are ends in themselves, everything else has its price, as is well reflected in the subjection in international law of environmental interdictions to military necessity. Even utilitarian defenders of animal rights need not attribute equal worth to humans and all other animals.[320]

Of course, all this may just beg the question from an anthropocentric stance, or at least a very inegalitarian bio-centric account. Some non-anthropocentric theorists construct deontological moral arguments that attribute inherent worth (intrinsic value), in whole or part, to non-human elements of the natural world[321] – an 'objective good-of-their-own'[322] – while many others reject this moral framework altogether, attributing intrinsic value to animals and ecosystems for very different reasons.[323] Perhaps we have reached a dead end. The concept of terrorism as we know it from Maximillian Robespierre, from 9/11 to October 7, is admittedly human-centred. As is also its categorical condemnation from a liberal 'humanistic' perspective and even its defence by Western apologists of terrorism.[324] In this context, so called 'environmental terrorism' runs the risk of abusing the concept of terrorism for rhetorical purposes, discrediting the absoluteness of the liberal prohibition on terror as well as the reasons for it that attach specifically to the value of human life, *imago Dei*, and the inherent worth of individual human persons.

4.4 Appropriate Response: The Case of Gaza and Beyond

Terrorism or no terrorism, no state can tolerate violent attacks on its territory and natural resources, alongside the property and ecological losses that accompany both. Regarding the natural environment per se, occasionally referred to as war's 'forgotten victim', some lawyers support a Fifth Geneva Convention on the Protection of the Environment in Time of Armed Conflict.[325] Others propose the criminalization of 'ecocide', either domestically – specifically referring to 'environmental terrorism'[326] – or more recently as an international war crime.[327] Any of this might go part way towards remedying current

---

[319] Kant, 1964: 96; Rawls, 1989: 179. [320] For example, Singer, 2011: 279, 281–82.
[321] For example, Drucker, 1989; Regan, 1986. [322] Taylor, 1986: 71–72, 77.
[323] For example, Attfield, 2005; Callicott, 1989; 2016; Leopold, 1980.
[324] For example Honderich, 1989; 2002; Chomsky, 2001.
[325] Plant, 1992; Seacor, 1994: esp. 507, 520–22. [326] Schofield, 1999: 645–46
[327] Sands and Sow, 2021.

inadequacies of legal protections, and expressly condemn the environmental nature of the crime.[328] Legal channels are, however, unlikely to offer immediate practical relief to nations suffering environmental assault.

What unilateral military measures might a state legitimately resort to in order to fend off environmental attacks? This question was hotly debated in connection with the inflammatory kites and balloons from Gaza. As with 'environmental terrorism' more generally, formulating appropriate and effective responses to this new threat was not easy.[329] Two key issues applied to the particularities of the Gaza case. The first concerned the overall legal framework of the arson attacks (armed conflict governed by international humanitarian law, or domestic law enforcement). The second questioned the legal status of the incendiary weapons launchers: were they in fact Hamas operatives or independent violent rioters?[330] Fighting Hamas terrorism from Gaza under the auspices of armed conflict is one thing; shooting at teenagers flying a kite is quite another. Israel steadfastly maintained the former approach, but nonetheless struggled at that time with an appropriate response. 'Technological non-lethal solutions for thwarting the kites, such as drones deflecting the kites from their trajectory, are not an ultimate solution; and options other than the use of lethal force to thwart the threat, such as talks and warnings, have proved useless.'[331] One cannot in good faith target children, limiting the level of force against the actual imminent threat to something like a law-enforcement operation or self-defence.[332]

The more permissive hostility model widened legitimate targets to Hamas personnel and assets, rather than merely responding to the immediate threat, namely the incendiary apparatus and its launchers, who were mostly youngsters.[333] The armed conflict model allowed Israel to target the leaders of Hamas, particularly its military wing, as well as weapons factories and warehouses, in response to the damage wrought upon Israeli territory, in the hope of reducing the risk and deterring future attacks.

Though Hamas may not have initiated the 'kite-unit', it quickly endorsed and adopted its fire attacks as an attractive tactic, supported and encouraged them, turning the kite/balloon-based arson into a central operation effort.[334] While launchers may or may not have received direct orders, Hamas clearly exploited these weaponized kites and balloons for its terroristic purposes.[335] There is no

---

[328] Schofield, 1999: 646.   [329] Compare Chalecki, 2002: 62.
[330] Moodrick-Even Khen, 2019: 329–34; Stefanini, 2021: 669, 672–73; Zych, 2019: 75.
[331] Moodrick-Even Khen, 2019: 332.   [332] Moodrick-Even Khen, 2019: 333.
[333] Moodrick-Even Khen, 2019: 332–34.
[334] Moodrick-Even Khen, 2019: 330–31; Stefanini, 2021: 669–70; Yadlin, 2018: 2; Zych, 2019: 75.
[335] Zych, 2019: esp. 72–73, 76–9.

doubt that between 2018 and Fall 2023 Hamas exercised full effective authority over the Gaza Strip, and at times adopted the fire attacks as its own with threats to keep the kite launch going.[336] The low-tech weapons not only served the Hamas government's public image but also enabled it to attack Israel while maintaining deniability and avoiding full-scale kinetic warfare, in which Israel clearly has the upper hand and which both parties appeared to have been avoiding at the time.[337]

The Gaza case study has since been overtaken by events, but it remains a recent and quite singular paradigm of 'environmental terrorism' associated with a recognized terrorist group and re-raises the wider issue of combatting environmental aggression. Section 2 argued that limiting counter-measures to the use of force short of full-scale war should avoid the pitfall of generating more environmental damage than protection, outweighing the environmental benefits of the response. Confronting the incendiary objects from Gaza, Israel used a mixture of 'smart weapons', such as precision rifles, optical tracking systems, and laser blades to detect and deflate airborne balloons and to grapple and bring down kites, as well as economic sanctions, with only partial success at halting and preventing attacks.[338] Pre-emptive military measures, such as surgical drone strikes against weapons facilities and targeted killings of those responsible, may be more effective against arson attacks.[339]

Regarding Gaza, in hindsight, all efforts to repel and deter Hamas aggression proved tragically unsuccessful. Notwithstanding and more generally, from both human- and non-human-centred perspectives, resorting to *jus ad vim* against purely environmental aggression is probably our best shot in terms of efficacy and proportionality. This sets 'environmental terrorism' and the appropriate response to it wholly apart from physical invasion and outright terrorism against civilians, even when the two appear in retrospect as points on a single continuum.

4.5 Concluding Remarks

While the underlying phenomenon of environmental destruction during armed conflict is an old story, the deliberate use of this tactic by terrorist organizations, like the scholarly study of 'environmental terrorism', remains in its infancy. Early twenty-first-century academia saw a multidisciplinary surge of interest in the study of terrorism. Typical definitions emphasize non-combatant targets, illegality, political motivation, generating fear, and 'theatre' influencing an

---

[336] Moodrick-Even Khen, 2019: 330–1.
[337] Stefanini, 2021: 674; Yadlin, 2018; Zych, 2019: 78–79.
[338] Stefanini, 2021: 673; Yadlin, 2018: 3; Zych, 2019: 80–81.   [339] Compare Zych, 2019: 80.

audience. While every element is contestable, all definitions and descriptions assume human targets.

As we face unprecedented environmental degradation on many fronts, the harm done by terroristic attacks to natural resources – deliberately destroying ecosystems and natural habitats – exceeds the immediate damage to property and human well-being. Nonetheless, the use of the term 'terrorism' in this context seems mostly a matter of political polemic. Extending absolute civilian immunity to non-human elements of the natural world, condemning any attack on the environment or its use as 'terrorism', is rather a stretch. At least from the perspectives of our current political philosophies, this derogatory label applies primarily to human victims.

Attaching the terrorism label to ecological destruction runs the risk of belittling human suffering and the inherent worth of human life, though this argument admittedly prompts the question of anthropocentric ethics. The issue of whether humanity is increasingly progressing towards the recognition of other inhabitants of the earth as equivalent in their intrinsic value exceeds the scope of this essay. Targeting the environment exclusively does not qualify as terrorism by most existing accounts of it and cannot warrant the type of military response or unequivocal condemnation that liberal morality attaches to terrorist strikes, particularly in terms of Kantian interdictions on using human beings as means only and on free riding.

Two caveats: none of the above diminishes or detracts from the severity of attacking the natural environment, the gravity of harm caused, or the need to respond. Moreover, in all likelihood, environmental attacks will often prejudice civilian populations quite directly, as is well reflected in the laws of war. Attacks on the natural environment may not discriminate between human and non-human targets; they may target human non-combatants within the environment; destroy essential resources; ignite, pollute, or contaminate civilian surroundings, and so forth, or represent one link in a terroristic chain of events.

The arson attacks emanating from the Gaza Strip on the Israeli South presented a useful case study of 'environmental terrorism' up to Fall 2023. The rest is history. In this case, the applicability of the terrorism label is a moot point. From forests to falcons, incendiary attacks not only impacted but also targeted non-combatants, particularly children. Like Hamas's inaccurate rockets, their initial lack of success in trying to kill Israelis does not excuse them from the charge of terrorism. The worst was yet to come.

Even where the harm inflicted is purely environmental, no state can indefinitely ignore attacks on their natural resources. Beyond putting out fires, arson attacks require a response. Classifying environmental attacks either as local crimes or as armed conflict, as well as identifying their perpetrators as civilians or irregular combatants directly engaged in hostilities, forms the crux of appropriate reaction. Where non-kinetic tactics have been exhausted and military response is apt and necessary, environmental and humanitarian concerns make a case for limited counter-measures – the use of pinpointed military force, short of war – against primary culprits and their infrastructure, at least as a first call, reserving full-scale armed conflict to combatting invasion and murderous attacks.

References

Akande, Dapo. 2012. Classification of Armed Conflicts: Relevant Legal Concepts. In Elizabeth Wilmshurst (ed.), *International Law and the Classification of Conflicts*. Oxford University Press, pp. 32–79.

Alex, Bastien and Adrien Estève. 2018. Defense Stakeholders and Climate Change: A Chronicle of a New Strategic Constraint in France and the United States. *Revue internationale et stratégique* 109(10): 93–103.

Aristotle. 1976. *The Nicomachean Ethics*. London: Penguin Classics.

Attfield, Robin. 2005. Biocentric Consequentialism and Value-Pluralism: A Response to Alan Carter. *Utilitas* 17(1): 85–92.

Attfield, Robin. 2018. *Environmental Ethics: A Very Short Introduction*. Oxford University Press.

Avdoshyn, I., M. Velychko, O. Kyryliuk, and M. Kryvych. 2019. Russian Military Aggression against Ukraine through the Prism of Hazard of Hostile Military and Anthropogenic Influence on Environment. *One Health and Nutrition Problems of Ukraine* 51(2): 5–11.

Berman, Paul. 2003. *Terror and Liberalism*. New York: W. W. Norton.

Betz, Adam. 2019. Preventive Environmental Wars. *Journal of Military Ethics* 18(3): 223–47.

Borradori, Giovanna. 2003. *Philosophy in a Time of Terror: Dialogues with Jurgen Habermas and Jacques Derrida*. The University of Chicago Press.

Bruch, Carl E. 2001. All's Not Fair in (Civil) War: Criminal Liability for Environmental Damage in Internal Armed Conflict. *Vermont Law Review* 25(3): 695–752.

Brunstetter, Daniel and Megan Braun. 2013. From *Jus ad Bellum* to *Jus ad Vim*: Recalibrating Our Understanding of the Moral Use of Force. *Ethics and International Affairs* 27(1): 87–106.

Burger, James A. 1996. Environmental Aspects of Non-International Conflicts: The Experience in Former-Yugoslavia. In Richard J. Grunawalt EE, John E. King, and Ronald S. McClain (eds), *Protection of the Environment during Armed Conflict*. Vol. 69 of International Law Studies. Newport, RI: U.S. Naval War College, pp. 333–45.

Callicott, J. Baird. 1989. *In Defense of the Land Ethic: Essays in Environmental Philosophy*. State University of New York Press.

Callicott, J. Baird. 2016. How Ecological Collectives Are Morally Considerable. In Stephen M. Gardiner and Allen Thompson (eds), *The Oxford Handbook of Environmental Ethics*. Oxford University Press, pp. 113–24.

Caney, Simon. 2015. Responding to Global Injustice: On the Right of Resistance. *Social Philosophy and Policy* 32(1): 51–73.

Cassese, Antonio. 2008. *The Human Dimension of International Law: Selected Papers of Antonio Cassese*. Oxford University Press.

Chalecki, Elizabeth L. 2002. A New Vigilance: Identifying and Reducing the Risks of Environmental Terrorism. *Global Environmental Politics* 2(1): 46–64.

Chomsky, Noam. 2001. *9–11*. New York: Seven Stories Press.

Coady, C. A. J. 2001. Terrorism. In Lawrence C. Becker and Charlotte B. Becker (eds), *Encyclopedia of Ethics*. 2nd ed. New York: Routledge.

Coady, C. A. J. 2004. Defining Terrorism. In Igor Primoratz (ed.), *Terrorism: The Philosophical Issues*. London: Palgrave Macmillan, pp. 3–14.

Cohan, John Alan. 2002. Modes of Warfare and Evolving Standards of Environmental Protection under the International Law of War. *Florida Journal of International Law* 15: 481–539.

Collier, Paul and Anke Hoeffler. 2004. Greed and Grievance in Civil War. *Oxford Economic Papers* 56(4): 563–95.

Collier, Paul, Lani Elliott, Håvard Hegre, Anke Hoeffler, Marta Reynal-Querol, and Nicholas Sambanis. 2003. *Breaking the Conflict Trap: Civil War and Development Policy*. Oxford University Press.

Crawford, Neta C. 2022. *The Pentagon, Climate Change, and War: Charting the Rise and Fall of US Military Emissions*. Cambridge, MA: MIT Press.

Cullen, Anthony. 2010. *The Concept of Non-International Armed Conflict in International Humanitarian Law*. Cambridge University Press.

Dahman, Ibrahim, Kareem Khadder, and Hadas Gold. 2023. Israel Strikes Gaza Targets after Incendiary Balloons Sent across Border. *CNN*, 23 September.

Daskin, Joshua H. and Robert M. Pringle. 2018. Warfare and Wildlife Declines in Africa's Protected Areas. *Nature* 553: 328–32.

Daskin, Joshua H., Marc Stalmans, and Robert M. Pringle. 2016. Ecological Legacies of Civil War: 35-Year Increase in Savanna Tree Cover following Wholesale Large-Mammal Declines. *Journal of Ecology* 104(1): 79–89.

Deiderich, Michael D., Jr. 1992. "Law of War" and Ecology: A Proposal for a Workable Approach to Protecting the Environment through the Law of War. *Military Law Review* 136: 137–60.

De-Shalit, Avner. 1995. *Why Posterity Matters: Environmental Policies and Future Generations*. Environmental Philosophies Series. London: Routledge.

Dinstein, Yoram. 2016. *The Conduct of Hostilities under the Law of International Armed Conflict*. Cambridge University Press.

Drucker, Merrit P. 1989. The Military Commander's Responsibility for the Environment. *Environmental Ethics* 11(2): 135–52.

Dudley, Joseph P., Joshua R. Ginsberg, Andrew J. Plumptre, John A. Hart, and Liliana C. Campos. 2002. Effects of War and Civil Strife on Wildlife and Wildlife Habitats. *Conservation Biology* 16(2): 319–29.

Eckersley, Robyn. 2007. Ecological Intervention: Prospects and Limits. *Ethics & International Affairs* 21(3): 293–316.

Edgerton, Laura. 1992. Eco-Terrorist Acts during the Persian Gulf War: Is International Law Sufficient to Hold Iraq Liable? *Georgia Journal of International and Comparative Law* 22: 151–74.

Estève, Adrien. 2020. Reflecting on the Protection of the Natural Environment in Times of War: The Contribution of the Just War Tradition. Translated by Robin Mackay. *Raisons politiques* 77(1): 55–65.

Fabre, Cécile. 2012. *Cosmopolitan War*. Oxford University Press.

Fabre, Cécile. 2021. Territorial Sovereignty and Humankind's Common Heritage. *Journal of Social Philosophy* 52(1): 17–23.

Fearon, James D. 2004. Why Do Some Civil Wars Last So Much Longer than Others? *Journal of Peace Research* 41(3): 275–301.

Fearon, James D. and David D. Laitin. 2003. Ethnicity, Insurgency, and Civil War. *American Political Science Review* 97(1): 75–90.

Fletcher, George, P. 2006. The Indefinable Concept of Terrorism. *Journal of International Criminal Justice* 4(5): 1–18.

Forge, John. 2009. Proportionality, Just War Theory and Weapons Innovation. *Science and Engineering Ethics* 15: 25–38.

Gardam, Judith. 1993. Proportionality and Force in International Law. *American Journal of International Law* 87: 391–413.

Gardam, Judith. 2004. *Necessity, Proportionality and the Use of Force by States*. Cambridge University Press.

Gardam, Judith. 2005. A Role for Proportionality in the War on Terror. *Nordic Journal of International Law* 74: 3–25.

Gilbert, Paul. 2003. *New Terror, New Wars*. Edinburgh University Press.

Gleick, Peter H. 2014. Water, Drought, Climate Change, and Conflict in Syria. *Weather, Climate, and Society* 6(3): 331–40.

Goodin, Robert E. 2006. *What's Wrong with Terrorism?* Cambridge, UK: Polity Press.

Green, Leslie C. 2018. *The Contemporary Law of Armed Conflict*. 3rd ed. Manchester University Press.

Grey, Christine. 2008. *International Law and the Use of Force*. 3rd ed. Oxford University Press.

Gross, Michael L. 2015. *The Ethics of Insurgency: A Critical Guide to Just Guerrilla Warfare*. New York: Oxford University Press.

Gross, Michael L. and Tamar Meisels (eds) 2017. *Soft War: The Ethics of Unarmed Conflict*. New York: Cambridge University Press.

Grotius, Hugo. 1625/2012. *The Rights of War and Peace*. Cambridge University Press.

Hanson, Thor. 2018. Biodiversity Conservation and Armed Conflict: A Warfare Ecology Perspective. *Annals of the New York Academy of Sciences* 1429(1): 50–65.

Hanson, Thor, Thomas M. Brooks, Gustavo A. B. Da Fonseca, Michael Hoffmann, John F. Lamoreux, Gary Machlis, Cristina G. Mittermeier, Russell A. Mittermeier, and John D. Pilgrim. 2009. Warfare in Biodiversity Hotspots. *Conservation Biology* 23(3): 578–87.

Hedahl, Marcus and Kyle Fruh. 2019. Climate Change as Unjust War. *Southern Journal of Philosophy* 57: 378–401.

Hedahl, Marcus, Scott Clark, and Michael Beggins. 2017. The Changing Nature of the Just War Tradition: How Our Changing Environment Ought to Change the Foundations of Just War Theory. *Public Integrity* 19(5): 429–43.

Held, Virginia. 2004. Terrorism, Rights and Political Goals. In Igor Primoratz (ed.), *Terrorism: The Philosophical Issues*. London: Palgrave Macmillan, pp. 66–79.

Henderson, Errol A. and J. David Singer. 2000. Civil War in the Post-Colonial World, 1946–92. *Journal of Peace Research* 37(3): 275–99.

Hiller, Avram. 2016. Consequentialism in Environmental Ethics. In Stephen M. Gardiner and Allen Thompson (eds), *The Oxford Handbook of Environmental Ethics*. Oxford University Press, pp. 199–210.

Homer-Dixon, Thomas F. 1991. On the Threshold: Environmental Changes as Causes of Acute Conflict. *International Security* 16(2): 76–116.

Homer-Dixon, Thomas F. 1994. Environmental Scarcities and Violent Conflict: Evidence from Cases. *International Security* 19(1): 5–40.

Honderich, Ted. 1989. *Terrorism for Humanity: Inquiries in Political Philosophy*. London: Pluto Press.

Honderich, Ted. 2002. *After the Terror*. Edinburgh University Press.

Hourcle, Laurent R. 2001. Environmental Law of War. *Vermont Law Review* 25(3): 653–93.

Hurka, Thomas. 2005. Proportionality in the Morality of War. *Philosophy & Public Affairs* 33(1): 34–66.

ICRC (International Committee of the Red Cross). 2019. How Nature Is Protected during Conflict: The Laws of War. www.youtube.com/watch?v=vTJCk41Qowo.

Ide, Tobias. 2018. Climate War in the Middle East? Drought, the Syrian Civil War and the State of Climate-Conflict Research. *Current Climate Change Reports* 4(4): 347–54.

Jensen, Eric Talbot. 2005. Of Environmental Warfare: Active and Passive Damage during Armed Conflict. *Vanderbilt Journal of Transnational Law* 38: 145–86.

Johnston, Laurie. 2015. Just War Theory and Environmental Destruction. In Tobias Winright and Laurie Johnston (eds), *Can War Be Just in the 21st Century: Ethicists Engage the Tradition*. Maryknoll, NY: Orbis Books.

Johnston, Laurie. 2016. *The Boisi Center Interviews*, No. 120. 17 March.

Kalyvas, Stathis N. 2006. *The Logic of Violence in Civil War*. Cambridge University Press.

Kalyvas, Stathis N. 2009. Civil War. In Carles Boix and Susan C. Stokes (eds), *The Oxford Handbook of Comparative Politics*. Oxford University Press, pp. 416–35.

Kant, Immanuel. 1964. *Groundwork of the Metaphysic of Morals*. Translated and Analysed by H. J. Paton. New York: Harper & Row.

Kanyamibwa, Samuel. 1998. Impact of War on Conservation: Rwandan Environment and Wildlife in Agony. *Biodiversity & Conservation* 7(11): 1399–406.

Kasher, Asa. 2009. Operation Cast Lead and the Ethics of Just War. *AZURE*, No. 37: 43–75. www.azure.org.il/article.php?id=502&page=all.

Kikuta, Kyosuke. 2020. The Environmental Costs of Civil War: A Synthetic Comparison of the Congolese Forests with and without the Great War of Africa. *The Journal of Politics* 82(4): 1243–55.

Koubi, Vally. 2019. Climate Change and Conflict. *Annual Review of Political Science* 22: 343–360.

Lacina, Bethany. 2006. Explaining the Severity of Civil Wars. *Journal of Conflict Resolution* 50(2): 276–89.

Laqueur, Walter Z. 1987. *The Age of Terrorism*. Boston: Little Brown and Company.

Lazar, Seth. 2010. Necessity, Vulnerability, and Noncombatant Immunity. Unpublished Manuscript. Cited with permission from the author.

Lazar, Seth. 2017. Just War Theory: Revisionists Versus Traditionalists. *Annual Review of Political Science* 20(1): 37–54.

Leader, Stefan H. and Peter Probst. 2003. The Earth Liberation Front and Environmental Terrorism. *Terrorism and Political Violence* 15(4): 37–58.

Lee, Sarah. 1991. A Geneva Convention for the Environment. *The Solicitors' Journal* 135: 386.

Lee, Stephen P. 2012. *Ethics and War: An Introduction*. Cambridge University Press.

Leiser, Burton M. 1986. Enemies of Mankind. In Benjamin Netanyahu (ed.), *Terrorism: How the West Can Win*. New York: Farrar, Straus and Giroux, pp. 155–56.

Leiser, Burton M. 2004. The Catastrophe of September 11 and Its Aftermath. In Igor Primoratz, *Terrorism: The Philosophical Issues*. London: Palgrave Macmillan, pp. 192–208.

Leopold, Aldo. 1980. *A Sand County Almanac, and Sketches Here and There*. Oxford University Press.

Licklider, Roy. 1995. The Consequences of Negotiated Settlements in Civil Wars, 1945–1993. *American Political Science Review* 89(3): 681–87.

Lindsell, Jeremy A., Erik Klop, and Alhaji M. Siaka. 2011. The Impact of Civil War on Forest Wildlife in West Africa: Mammals in Gola Forest, Sierra Leone. *Oryx* 45(1): 69–77.

Loadenthal, Michael. 2017. 'Eco-Terrorism': An Incident-Driven History of Attack (1973–2010). *Journal for the Study of Radicalism* 11(2): 1–34.

Luban, David. 2013. Risk Taking and Force Protection. In Yitzhak Benbaji and Naomi Sussman (eds), *Reading Walzer*. London: Routledge, pp. 277–301.

Machlis, Gary E. and Thor Hanson. 2008. Warfare Ecology. *BioScience* 58(8): 729–36.

Martin, Craig. 2020. Atmospheric Intervention? The Climate Change Crisis and the *Jus ad Bellum* Regime. *Columbia Journal of Environmental Law* 45(2): 332–417.

Mason, T. David and Patrick J. Fett. 1996. How Civil Wars End: A Rational Choice Approach. *Journal of Conflict Resolution* 40(4): 546–68.

McMahan, Jeff. 2004. The Ethics of Killing in War. *Ethics* 114(4): 693–733.

McMahan, Jeff. 2005. Just Cause for War. *Ethics & International Affairs* 19(3): 1–21.

McMahan, Jeff. 2008. The Morality of War and the Law of War. In David Rodin and Henry Shue (eds), *Just and Unjust Warriors: The Moral and Legal Status of Soldiers*. New York: Oxford University Press, pp. 19–43.

McMahan, Jeff. 2009. *Killing in War*. Oxford University Press.

McMahan, Jeff. 2012. Rethinking the 'Just War', Part 2. *The New York Times*, 11 November. https://archive.nytimes.com/opinionator.blogs.nytimes.com/2012/11/11/,rethinking-the-just-war-part-1/.

McMahan, Jeff. 2020. Climate Change, War, and the Non-identity Problem. *Journal of Moral Philosophy* 18(3): 211–38.

McMahan, Jeff and Robert Mckin. 1993. The Just War and the Gulf War. *Canadian Journal of Philosophy* 23: 501–41.

Meisels, Tamar. 2006. The Trouble with Terror: The Apologetics of Terrorism: A Refutation. *Terrorism and Political Violence* 18(3): 465–83.

Meisels, Tamar. 2008. *The Trouble with Terror: Liberty, Security and the Response to Terrorism.* Cambridge University Press.

Meisels Tamar. 2009. Defining Terrorism: A Typology. *Critical Review of International Social and Political Philosophy* 12(3): 331–51.

Meisels, Tamar. 2012. In Defense of the Defenseless: The Morality of the Laws of War. *Political Studies* 60(4): 919–35.

Meisels, Tamar. 2017. *Contemporary Just War: Theory and Practice.* London: Routledge.

Meron, Theodor. 1996. Comment: Protection of the Environment during Non-international Armed Conflict. In Richard J. Grunawalt, John E. King, and Ronald S. McClain (eds), *Protection of the Environment during Armed Conflict.* Vol. 69 of International Law Studies. Newport, RI: U.S. Naval War College, pp. 353–58.

Milburn, Josh and Sara Van Goozen. 2021. Counting Animals in War: First Steps towards an Inclusive Just-War Theory. *Social Theory & Practice* 47(4): 657–85.

Milburn, Josh & Sara Van Goozen. 2023. Animals and the Ethics of War: A Call for an Inclusive Just-War Theory. *International Relations* 37(3): 423–48.

Moodrick-Even Khen, Hilly. 2019. From Knives to Kites: Developments and Dilemmas around the Use of Force in the Israeli–Palestinian Conflict since 'Protective Edge'. *Journal of International Humanitarian Legal Studies* 10: 303–36.

Murillo-Sandoval, Paulo J., Emma Gjerdseth, Camilo Correa-Ayram, David Wrathall, Jamon Van Den Hoek, Liliana M. Dávalos, and Robert Kennedy. 2021. No Peace for the Forest: Rapid, Widespread Land Changes in the Andes-Amazon Region following the Colombian Civil War. *Global Environmental Change* 69: 102–83.

Netanyahu, Benjamin (ed.). 1986. *Terrorism: How the West Can Win.* New York: Farrar, Straus and Giroux.

Netanyahu, Benjamin. 2001. *Fighting Terrorism.* 2nd ed. New York: Farrar, Straus and Giroux.

Nine, Cara. 2022. *Sharing Territories: Overlapping Self-determination and Resource Rights.* New Topics in Applied Philosophy. Oxford University Press.

Nolt, John. 2016. Future Generations in Environmental Ethics. In Stephen M. Gardiner and Allen Thompson (eds), *The Oxford Handbook of Environmental Ethics.* Oxford University Press, pp. 344–56.

O'Lear, Shannon. 2003. Environmental Terrorism: A Critique. *Geopolitics* 8(3): 127–50.

Parry, Jonathan. 2015. Civil War and Revolution. In Seth Lazar and Helen Frowe (eds), *The Oxford Handbook of Ethics and War*. Oxford University Press, pp. 315–36.

Plant, Glen. 1992. *Environmental Protection and the Law of War: A 'Fifth Geneva' Convention on the Environment in Time of Armed Conflict?* London: Belhaven Press.

Primoratz, Igor (ed.). 2004. *Terrorism: The Philosophical Issues*. London: Palgrave Macmillan.

Rawls, John. 1989. *A Theory of Justice*. 9th ed. New York: Oxford University Press.

Rawls, John. 2005. *Political Liberalism*: Expanded Edition. New York: Columbia University Press.

Rawtani, Deepak, Gunjan Gupta, Nitasha Khatri, Piyush K. Rao, and Chaudhery Mustansar Hussain. 2022. Environmental Damages due to War in Ukraine: A Perspective. *Science of the Total Environment* 850: 157932.

Regan, Patrick M. 2002. Third-Party Interventions and the Duration of Intrastate Conflicts. *Journal of Conflict Resolution* 46(1): 55–73.

Regan, Tom. 1986. The Case for Animal Rights. In M. W. Fox and L. D. Mickley (eds), *Advances in Animal Welfare Science*. Washington, DC: The Humane Society of the United States, pp. 179–89.

Reichberg, Gregory M. and Henrik Syse. 2000. Protecting the Natural Environment in Wartime: Ethical Considerations from the Just War Tradition. *Journal of Peace Research* 37(4): 449–68.

Richards, Peter J. and Michael N. Schmitt. 1999. Mars Meets Mother Nature: Protecting the Environment during Armed Conflict. *Stetson Law Review* 28(4): 1047–90.

Roberts, Adam. 1996. Environmental Issues in International Armed Conflict: The Experience of the 1991 Gulf War. *International Law Studies* 69: 222–77.

Roberts, Adam. 2000. The Law of War and Environmental Damage. In Jay E. Austin and Carl E. Bruch (eds), *The Environmental Consequences of War*. Cambridge University Press, pp. 47–86.

Rodin, David. 2003. *War and Self-defense*. Oxford University Press.

Sands, Philippe and Dior Fall Sow. 2021. Independent Expert Panel for the Legal Definition of Ecocide, Stop Ecocide Foundation.

Schmid, Alex P. 1984. *Political Terrorism: A Research Guide to Concepts, Theories, Data Bases and Literature*. Amsterdam: North Holland Publishing Company.

Schmid, Alex P. and Janny de Graaf. 1982. *Violence as Communication: Insurgent Terrorism and the Western News Media*. London: Sage.

Schmid, Alex P. and Albert J. Jongman. 1988. *Political Terrorism: A Research Guide to Concepts, Theories, Data Bases and Literature*. 2nd ed. Amsterdam: North Holland Publishing Company.

Schmitt, Michael N. 1996. The Environmental Law of War: An Invitation to Critical Reexamination. *USAFA Journal of Legal Studies* 6: 237–71.

Schmitt, Michael N. 1997. Green War: An Assessment of the Environmental Law of International Armed Conflict. *Yale Journal of International Law* 22(1): 1–109.

Schofield, Timothy. 1999. The Environment as an Ideological Weapon: Proposal to Criminalize Environmental Terrorism. *Boston College Environmental Affairs Law Review* 26(3): 619–48.

Schwabach, Aaron. 2000. Environmental Damage Resulting from the NATO Military Action against Yugoslavia. *Columbia Journal of Environmental Law* 25(1): 117–40.

Schwabach, Aaron. 2003. Ecocide and Genocide in Iraq: International Law, the Marsh Arabs and Environmental Damage in Non-international Conflicts. TJSL Public Law Research Paper, No. 03–08, 1–37.

Schwartz, Daniel M. 1998. Environmental Terrorism: Analyzing the Concept. *Journal of Peace Research* 35(4): 483–96.

Scott, P. Eagan. 1996. From Spikes to Bombs: The Rise of Eco-terrorism. *Studies in Conflict and Terrorism* 19(1): 1–18.

Seacor, Jessica E. 1994. Environmental Terrorism: Lessons from the Oil Fires of Kuwait. *American University Journal of International Law and Policy* 10(1): 481–523.

Selby, Jan, Omar S. Dahi, Christiane Fröhlich, and Mike Hulme. 2017. Climate Change and the Syrian Civil War Revisited. *Political Geography* 60: 232–44.

Shue, Henry. 1978. Torture. *Philosophy and Public Affairs* 7(2): 124–43.

Shue, Henry. 2008. Do We Need a 'Morality of War'? In David Rodin and Henry Shue (eds), *Just and Unjust Warriors: The Moral and Legal Status of Soldiers*. New York: Oxford University Press, pp. 87–111.

Singer, Peter. 1974. All Animals Are Equal. *Philosophic Exchange* 1(5): 103–16.

Singer, Peter. 1977. Animal Liberation. *The New York Review of Books* 20(5): 1–8.

Singer, Peter. 1980. Utilitarianism and Vegetarianism. *Philosophy and Public Affairs* 9(4): 325–37.

Singer, Peter. 2000. *Writing on an Ethical Life*. New York: Ecco Press.

Singer, Peter. 2011. *Practical Ethics*. Cambridge University Press.

Smilansky, Saul. 2004. Terrorism, Justification, and Illusion. *Ethics* 114(4): 790–805.

Spadaro, Paola Andrea. 2020. Climate Change, Environmental Terrorism, Eco-terrorism and Emerging Threats. *Journal of Strategic Security* 13(4): 58–80.

Stefanini, Pietro. 2021. Incendiary Kites and Balloons: Anti-colonial Resistance in Palestine's Great March of Return. *Partecipazione e Conflitto – The Open Journal of Sociopolitical Studies* 14(2): 663–80.

Steffen, Lloyd. 2015. On War and the Environment: A Proposed Revision in the Ethics of Restraint. In Fiala Andres (ed.), *The Peace of Nature and the Nature of Peace: Essays on Ecology, Nature, Nonviolence, and Peace*. Leiden: Brill, pp. 41–50.

Taylor, Paul W. 1986. *Respect for Nature: A Theory of Environmental Ethics*. Studies in Moral, Political, and Legal Philosophy. Princeton University Press.

Tesón, Fernando R. 1995. Collective Humanitarian Intervention. *Michigan Journal of International Law* 17(2): 323–71.

Tesón, Fernando R. 2001. The Liberal Case for Humanitarian Intervention. https://ssrn.com/abstract=291661.

Tesón, Fernando R. 2006. Eight Principles for Humanitarian Intervention. *Journal of Military Ethics* 5(2): 93–113.

Times of Israel. 2018. In Worst Blaze to Date, Gaza Fire Kites Destroy Vast Parts of Nature Reserve. 2 June. www.timesofisrael.com/palestinian-fire-kites-destroy-much-of-nature-reserve-along-gaza-border/.

Ülker, Duygu, Orhan Ergüven, and Cem Gazioğlu. 2018. Socio-economic Impacts in a Changing Climate: Case Study Syria. *International Journal of Environment and Geoinformatics* 5(1): 84–93.

Vattel, Emerich de. 1758. *The Law of Nations or Principles of Natural Law Applied to the Conduct and Affairs of Nations and Sovereigns*. https://lonang.com/library/reference/vattel-law-of-nations/.

Vitoria, Francisco de. 1532/1991. *On the Law of War*. In F. de Vitoria, *Political Writings*. Translated by Anthony Pagden and Jeremy Lawrance. Cambridge University Press, pp. 293–327.

Waldron, Jeremy. 2004. Terrorism and the Uses of Terror. *The Journal of Ethics* 8: 5–35.

Waldron, Jeremy. 2010. *Torture, Terror, and Trade-Offs: Philosophy for the White House*. Oxford University Press.

Walter, Barbara F. 1997. The Critical Barrier to Civil War Settlement. *International Organization* 51(3): 335–64.

Walzer, Michael. 1977. *Just and Unjust Wars: A Moral Argument with Historical Illustrations*. New York: Basic Books.

Walzer, Michael. 2002. Five Questions about Terrorism. *Dissent* 49, No. 1, 5–11.

Walzer, Michael. 2004. *Arguing about War*. New Haven: Yale University Press.
Walzer, Michael. 2006a. *Just and Unjust Wars*. 4th ed. New York: Basic Books.
Walzer, Michael. 2006b. Terrorism and Just War. *Philosophia* 34: 3–12.
Watts, Susan. 1991. Environment Should Be Protected during War. *Independent*, 2 June.
Wenar, Leif. 2008. Property Rights and the Resource Curse. *Philosophy and Public Affairs* 36(1): 2–32.
Westing, Arthur H. 1983. The Environmental Aftermath of Warfare in Viet Nam. *Natural Resources Journal* 23(2): 365–89.
Westing, Arthur H. 1985. Environmental Warfare. *Environmental Law* 15(4): 645–66.
Wilkins, Burley Taylor. 1992. *Terrorism and Collective Responsibility*. London: Routledge.
Winright, Tobias and Laurie Johnston (eds). 2015. *Can War Be Just in the 21st Century? Ethicists Engage the Tradition*. Maryknoll, NY: Orbis Books.
Woods, Mark. 2007. The Nature of War and Peace: Just War Thinking, Environmental Ethics, and Environmental Justice. In Michael W. Brough, John W. Lango, and Harry van der Linden (eds), *Rethinking the Just War Tradition*. University of New York Press, pp. 17–34.
Yadlin, Amos. 2018. *On Deterrence, Equations, Arrangements, and Strategy*. Institute for National Security Studies. www.jstor.com/stable/resrep19437.
Young, Robert. 2004. Political Terrorism as a Weapon of the Politically Powerless. In Igor Primoratz (ed.), *Terrorism: The Philosophical Issues*. London: Palgrave Macmillan, pp. 55–64.
Zych, Joanna. 2019. The Use of Weaponised Kites and Balloons in the Israeli-Palestinian Conflict. *Security and Defense Quarterly* 27(5): 71–83.

Treaties and Conventions Cited

Antarctic Treaty (4 October 1991). Protocol on Environmental Protection. Articles 2–3. Entered into force 14 January 1998.
Conventions on Prohibitions or Restrictions on the Use of Certain Weapons Which May Be Deemed to Be Excessively Injurious or to Have Indiscriminate Effects (Protocol III) (10 October 1980). Article 2(4). Entered into force 2 December 1983.
Environmental Modification Convention (18 May 1977). Convention on the Prohibition of Military or Any Other Hostile Use of Environmental Modification Techniques. Entered into force 5 October 1978.
Geneva Conventions. Protocol Additional to the Geneva Conventions of 12 August 1949 and Relating to the Protection of Victims of International

Armed Conflicts (Protocol I) (8 June 1977). Articles 35(3), 55(1). Entered into force 7 December 1978.

Geneva Convention (III) Relative to the Treatment of Prisoners of War, Geneva (12 August 1949): Conflicts Not of an International Character.

Protocol Additional to the Geneva Conventions of 12 August 1949 and Relating to the Protection of Victims of Non-International Armed Conflicts (Protocol II) (8 June 1977).

Rome Statute of the International Criminal Court (19 July 1998). Article 8(2)(b)(iv). Entered into force 1 July 2002.

United Nations Convention on the Law of the Sea 1982. https://www.un.org/depts/los/convention_agreements/texts/unclos/unclos_e.pdf

Additional Source

Intergovernmental Panel on Climate Change (IPCC). 2019. *Climate Change and Land: An IPCC Special Report on Climate Change, Desertification, Land Degradation, Sustainable Land Management, Food Security, and Greenhouse Gas Fluxes in Terrestrial Ecosystems.*

Acknowledgements

This book is made up of four relatively new topics, originally researched piecemeal. I am most grateful to Chaim Gans who first suggested I gather the various pieces into one comprehensive manuscript, and for encouraging me to do so.

Some of this material has been published previously in two individual articles: 'Environmental Ethics of War: Jus ad Bellum, Jus in Bello, and the Natural Environment', *Conatus – Journal of Philosophy*, 8(2) (2023), 399–429; and 'Environmental Just Wars: *Jus ad Bellum* and the Natural Environment', *Journal of Applied Philosophy* (2024). I thank the journals for permission to use these materials here.

All this research was supported by the Israel Science Foundation (Grant no. 217/22).

I am grateful to Kerry Bennett and Avery Kolers, editors of the *Journal of Applied Philosophy*, for their critical attention and detailed suggestions, which ultimately improved Section 2.

Azar Gat offered sharp insights at the start of this project, which have continued to guide me throughout. Michael Gross has been extremely generous, reading and commenting usefully on articles and sections along the way, as well as on the final manuscript.

Two former students who have since become friends and colleagues were also invaluably helpful. Tamar Caner taught me most of what I know about civil wars. I am indebted to her research on non-international armed conflicts and for her co-authorship of an article that formed Section 3, as well as her permission to use these materials here. Adi Levy graciously shared his expertise on violent and non-violent resistance, improving my work on environmental terrorism. Our collaboration on his paper on armed and unarmed environmental violence, as well as his comments on my own work, have significantly enriched Section 4.

Finally, to the young members of my family – my daughters Abigail and Martha, my nephews Aaron, Avner, and Joel, and my niece Ella – whose generation must contend with war in a deteriorating environment: may God help and keep you.

Cambridge Elements

International Relations

Series Editors

Jon C. W. Pevehouse
University of Wisconsin–Madison

Jon C. W. Pevehouse is the Mary Herman Rubinstein Professor of Political Science and Public Policy at the University of Wisconsin–Madison. He has published numerous books and articles in IR in the fields of international political economy, international organizations, foreign policy analysis, and political methodology. He is a former editor of the leading IR field journal, International Organization.

Tanja A. Börzel
Freie Universität Berlin

Tanja A. Börzel is the Professor of political science and holds the Chair for European Integration at the Otto-Suhr-Institute for Political Science, Freie Universität Berlin. She holds a PhD from the European University Institute, Florence, Italy. She is coordinator of the Research College "The Transformative Power of Europe," as well as the FP7-Collaborative Project "Maximizing the Enlargement Capacity of the European Union" and the H2020 Collaborative Project "The EU and Eastern Partnership Countries: An Inside-Out Analysis and Strategic Assessment." She directs the Jean Monnet Center of Excellence "Europe and its Citizens."

Edward D. Mansfield
University of Pennsylvania

Edward D. Mansfield is the Hum Rosen Professor of Political Science, University of Pennsylvania. He has published well over 100 books and articles in the area of international political economy, international security, and international organizations. He is Director of the Christopher H. Browne Center for International Politics at the University of Pennsylvania and former program co-chair of the American Political Science Association.

Editorial Team

International Relations Theory
Jeffrey T. Checkel, European University Institute, Florence

International Political Economy
Edward D. Mansfield, University of Pennsylvania
Stefanie Walter, University of Zurich

International Security
Jon C. W. Pevehouse, University of Wisconsin–Madison

International Organisations
Tanja A. Börzel, Freie Universität Berlin

About the Series

The Cambridge Elements Series in International Relations publishes original research on key topics in the field. The series includes manuscripts addressing international security, international political economy, international organizations, and international relations.

Cambridge Elements

International Relations

Elements in the Series

Peace in Digital International Relations: Prospects and Limitations
Oliver P. Richmond, Gëzim Visoka and Ioannis Tellidis

Regionalized Governance in the Global South
Brooke Coe and Kathryn Nash

Digital Globalization: Politics, Policy, and a Governance Paradox
Stephen Weymouth

After Hedging: Hard Choices for the Indo-Pacific States between the US and China
Kai He and Huiyun Feng

IMF Lending: Partisanship, Punishment, and Protest
M. Rodwan Abouharb and Bernhard Reinsberg

Building Pathways to Peace: State–Society Relations and Security Sector Reform
Nadine Ansorg and Sabine Kurtenbach

Drones, Force and Law: European Perspectives
David Hastings Dunn and Nicholas J. Wheeler With Jack Davies, Zeenat Sabur

The Selection and Tenure of Foreign Ministers Around the World
Hanna Bäck, Alejandro Quiroz Flores and Jan Teorell

Lockean Liberalism in International Relations
Alexandru V. Grigorescu and Claudio J. Katz

Tip-toeing through the Tulips with Congress: How Congressional Attention Constrains Covert Action
Dani Kaufmann Nedal and Madison V. Schramm

Social Cues: How the Liberal Community Legitimizes Humanitarian War
Jonathan A. Chu

Environmental Ethics of War
Tamar Meisels

A full series listing is available at www.cambridge.org/EIR

For EU product safety concerns, contact us at Calle de José Abascal, 56–1º, 28003 Madrid, Spain or eugpsr@cambridge.org.

www.ingramcontent.com/pod-product-compliance
Lightning Source LLC
LaVergne TN
LVHW020350260326
834688LV00045B/1652